500 Horror Writing Prompts

SLASHERS

CHRISTINA ESCAMILLA

Copyright © 2025 by Christina Escamilla

All rights reserved. This book or any portion thereof may not be reproduced or used without the author's permission.

Unless otherwise noted, this book's characters, names, places, and events are fictitious. Any mention of real-world characters, names, businesses, and events is made in an editorial facet. All information in this book is presented *as-is*. No representation or warranties surrounding further use of the information contained within this book have been drawn. The author and publisher shall not be liable for any endeavors taken up by these prompts in any degree whatsoever.

Check Out Other Writing Books by Christina Escamilla

Writing Prompts That Will Motivate You Creatively

1,001 Everyday Writing Prompts
1,001 Horror Writing Prompts
1,001 Sci-Fi Writing Prompts
1,001 Romance Writing Prompts

500 Horror Writing Prompts Series

500 Horror Writing Prompts: Monsters Unleashed
500 Horror Writing Prompts: Contagion
500 Horror Writing Prompts: Unholy Encounters
500 Horror Writing Prompts: Bloodlust
500 Horror Writing Prompts: Haunted House
500 Horror Writing Prompts: Slashers

Writing Guides and Workbooks

1,001 Questions to Help Flesh Out Your Character
366 Daily Writing Exercises
The Character Creation Workbook
The Little Guide to Fiction Writing

On Genre Fiction

Write Horror: Good Enough to Wake the Dead

TABLE OF CONTENTS

```
Introduction ..............................6
Suburban Stalkers .........................7
Nightmare Campgrounds ....................29
Twisted Families & Hidden Ties ...........52
Fanatics & Deadly Devotions ..............72
Urban Legends Come Alive .................96
Holiday Hellscapes ......................119
Survivors & Sequels .....................141
```

INTRODUCTION

There is some debate over which film introduced the slasher archetype to the collective psyche, but there is no doubt that it is synonymous with the killer craze of the 1970s. Earlier films like *M* (1931) and *Psycho* (1960), of course, featured killers hiding in plain sight, but it was films like *Halloween* (1978) that pinpointed the exact concept that continues to horrify audiences now – the fight for survival against an unstoppable force. Michael Myers cannot be reasoned with or detour from his goal. Quite simply, if he wants to kill you, he will.

The slasher narrative continued to evolve with this core concept at the helm. Dark figures like Jason Voorhees from *Friday the 13th* (1980) break the serenity of the otherwise peaceful Crystal Lake, while Freddy Krueger from *A Nightmare on Elm Street* (1984) invades the sanctity of sleep. Again, it shows that these killers, no matter what setting or end goal, are driven to the point where nothing but their singular need or want matters.

The pursuit of the

victim and the fear associated with being killed also play into our fears of being trapped, being betrayed, and ultimately, having no control over our own deaths. After all, the slasher archetype underlines the idea that no one is safe, even in the comfort of one's own home.

The prompts in these collections explore all facets of the slasher archetype, from those who use twisted psychological warfare to the cunning maniac who is always waiting and watching.

May these prompts drive your pen to craft unforgettable nightmares and test the razor's edge between terror and survival.

Suburban Stalkers

The most innocent setting can often mask the most chilling horror. Within the cozy façade of idyllic cul-de-sacs and manicured yards, a terror can lie dormant, waiting to strike when streetlights are low and guards are up. These prompts deal with ordinary suburban settings that become stalking grounds for killers who slip in unnoticed.

1. "Stay off my lawn...or else!" Your young character and their group of friends ignore the warnings of the cantankerous elderly neighbor. That is until other neighborhood children go missing.

2. Your babysitter character is hired to watch two angelic children. Once inside the home, your character notices odd footprints leading to a locked tool shed. As night falls, the footprints have disappeared, but there is now fogged breath on the window glass. It seems your character isn't the only one watching the children.

3. Your character is a bullied high schooler who is the target of scrutiny when fellow students go missing. While your character certainly has a vendetta against these popular teens, they are not behind the disappearances. Their best friend is.

4. Firefighters cast uneasy glances at one another while waiting for the dispatch alarm to ring. Sure enough, it does. Not only do they have a serial arsonist on their hands, but

this person is also a serial killer, leaving one body at each burned building. Little do any of the gathered know, but a fellow firefighter is behind it all.

5. Write a horror comedy in which a neighborhood watch begins to turn on each other after searching for a masked killer who has been stalking the community. Who is the killer, and how can you weave in comedic elements with plenty of bloodshed?

6. "You can trust me, can't you?" Your character's hands shake as they point the gun at their stepparent, who looks equally terrified. Someone has been responsible for murdering the neighbors, and everything points to this person. But what if your character is wrong?

7. Imagine a scenario in which a librarian notices someone hasn't returned their books and it's well past the due date. Finally, the books are returned overnight at the drop-off. When the librarian opens the book, the pages are filled with bloody handprints.

8. It has been months since a small-town murder has rocked the local community. Once the grisly scene is cleared, the caution tape, still blowing in the wind, is the only reminder of what happened. Then, the tape is moved, and another murder occurs. Then, another and another. Is the culprit a member of the police force or just toying with them?

9. Neighbors are frustrated by a noisy lawnmower whose sound can be heard at all hours. Finally, the community has had enough and is determined to discover what is behind the annoyance. That's when the first severed limbs begin to appear amongst the lawn clippings.

10. Imagine a horror story that occurs over the course of one night involving one jogger who must escape a trailing car. Will the jogger get away, or will they be the victim of the person, or persons, inside the vehicle?

11. When a child is murdered in the sleepy town, all fingers point to a bus driver, who was notorious for being a little rough around the edges. To clear their name, the bus driver goes on a quest to find the killer, but this will prove far more difficult than they ever imagined.

12. Neighbors are shocked at what lies in the garage, which has unwittingly been left open. Inside are piles upon piles of eerily personal items – children's bikes, prescription glasses, a collection of wallets, wedding rings, and even a bloody sneaker. It seems the homeowner is a serial killer.

13. Your character stares at the endless rows of greenery that surrounds them and wonders if they will make it out of the hedge maze alive. After a garden party goes awry, your character has unwittingly become a pawn in an evil game.

14. Imagine a scenario where burglar alarms begin going off every day. The alarm company continues to do their fixes and insists that someone has tripped the alarm, but no one is there. Finally, the family has had enough and disarms the security system completely. That's exactly what the killer wants.

15. It's storming, and your character uses the downpour to hide from a slasher who only recently moved in. Will your character manage to survive the night? Why has this killer targeted this community in the first place?

16. When a neighbor starts offering "safety inspections" for houses in the community, your character is the only one who is suspicious. Your character has every right to be because this person has nefarious intentions, even if no one else believes them.

17. Write a horror comedy in which the head of the HOA will ensure that the yard is cut to precisely four inches, no cars are parked in the driveaway, and all gutters are spotless – *or else*.

18. Garage doors are notorious access points for criminals. They can gain entry by using a universal garage door opener, and sometimes homeowners even forget to lock up when they leave. Write a story in which a slasher has entered the garage and is now waiting patiently for your character to return home.

19. Your character stares at the house across the street, entranced by the lone flickering light. This has been going on for a few days now, and your character is convinced they are being sent a message. That's because they are. It is Morse code, and when decoded, it reveals a countdown – to murder.

20. Write a scenario in which, during a cookout, someone discovers a panic room at the host house. Another person chimes in, "Oh, I have one too." Then another and another. This creates stunned silence for those who do not have their own panic room. What is the unspeakable reason these rooms were built – and by whom?

21. A gang of suburban dogs, from golden doodles to Scottish terriers are the only ones who stand between a slasher and their owners. You can decide whether this is a horror comedy and whether or not this canine crew prevails in the end.

22. What's scarier than one suburban killer? A whole group of them! When your character thinks they have escaped the slasher's knife, another menace in the neighborhood is around the corner.

23. "Don't be scared," Your character leans down and tries to comfort their children. "I promise everything will be okay." Your character deadbolts every door and boards every window. Seconds later, the whir of a chainsaw can be heard. Your character gulps, wondering if they can really keep their promise.

24. Imagine a scenario in which a block party covers the entire length of the street. Attendees turn up murdered one by one, and yet, the party continues, loud, pumping music and all.

25. A missing cat is the catalyst for this slasher tale. No, the cat isn't hurt, but write a story in which a serial slayer steals a feline, and

this will ultimately end up being their undoing.

26. Your character is a real estate agent who sells dream homes daily, but at night, your character visits unsuspecting clients and makes their home a living nightmare. How long until this real estate agent character is found and brought to justice?

27. Suppose a couple goes off on vacation leaving their house unoccupied for their cruise. Why, then, are the lights on at night? Why are there tire tracks on the driveway? The answer to these questions is simple – the couple never went on vacation and their slayer currently lives in their house.

28. "I see you." The same cryptic message is scrawled on every parked car in a small subdivision. At first, the ominous words are passed off as a prank, but then the video cameras are reviewed. It isn't a prank, and it isn't an outsider, but someone in the community has

sinister plans for each car they have tagged.

29. Imagine a scenario in which the most immaculate house in the neighborhood hides a cellar with tapes filled with "accidents" the local families are still trying to move on from. Your character stumbles across these tapes, creating the potential for the next "accident."

30. When a young student vanishes after walking just two blocks from the school, rumors spread wildly. Parents begin barricading their homes and insist on driving or walking their children. That is exactly what the killer wants – a scared population will be easier to fall into the trap this monster has laid out.

31. A neighborhood's chic streetlights clast warm glows on meticulously kept houses, but echoes of terror fill the air after dark. Someone has a key to every front door, and there is no telling who will be next.

32. Your character and a relative are trapped in a grocery store's freezer. Behind the cartons of milk and coffee creamer, they watch in horror as a mass murderer passes by, looking for more victims to slay. Why was this grocery store targeted, and will your character and their relative make it out alive?

33. "Look at this... it's a photograph!" Your character shows the group portrait they have just picked up to their friend. The two were exploring a storm drain when they stumbled across a suitcase of miscellaneous items. After studying the photo, the two realize with horror that each person is a missing person from the neighborhood.

34. Someone has been stalking the residents of an apartment complex. At first, it is walking behind victims and heavy breathing, then residents turn up murdered. After a few residents realize who it is, they band together to set booby traps for the killer, hoping to stop this monster before they too are murdered.

35. Your character's neighbor throws a dinner party, and your character is elated at having been invited. When your character arrives, they are immediately ushered into the kitchen. They realize their neighbor's sinister plans too late – your character is the dinner.

36. "They never saw the truth, but you will." Your character takes a step back at the finger pointed directly at them. A figure in a tattered mask stands before our character. What truth does this suburban slasher speak of?

37. Suppose a peeping tom is on the prowl in an otherwise quiet town. No, this prowler is not the slasher. But while spying on a neighbor's house, they witness one in the middle of a murder.

38. Create a narrative that mixes the suburban slasher with another horror subgenre. For instance, you can include a slasher possessed by the devil (religious horror), a slasher who kills under the cover of an alien attack (science fiction horror), or another subgenre of your choosing!

39. Your character wakes up to find their bedroom window open and footprints by the flowerbed. Naturally, they are concerned but tell themselves it is probably a neighbor kid playing or a teen fulfilling a dare. That night, they are awoken by the sound of a loud crash. Then, they discover handprints covering the bedroom walls.

40. Your character is trapped inside their smart house, and a slasher is toying with them. How did this murderer get in? Because they happened to have been the one who installed the high-tech security system.

41. Each night, wails emanate from a foreclosed property that has been vacant for years. Finally, the neighbors involve the police, who investigate and find nothing. Taking it upon themselves, a few neighbors break in and try to find the source of the sound. One of the police

officers is still inside the home because is they who are the killer.

42. Terrified glances are a stunning visual at the community town hall, indicating that something is amiss. Every neighbor has reported hearing strange noises at night. Residents assumed it was just a family of raccoons. But after hearing similar stories of feeling watched, items going missing, and a few people's unsettling security camera footage, everyone is aware of the truth—there is a stalker in the midst.

43. "Are you sure there isn't anything else you need?" Your character is beginning to feel uneasy. At first, they appreciated the kind handyman who offered free home repairs, but now this person doesn't seem eager to leave. Your character has every right to be afraid. Unbeknownst to them, this handyman has been installing secret entrances and hidden cameras.

44. Imagine a scenario in which your character, the head of the HOA, demands an inspection of a house that is constantly reported.

Surprisingly, the recluse homeowner obliges. Once inside, your character is horrified – the house is a labyrinth of one-way glass, with each panel pointed to the bedrooms of unsuspecting neighbors.

45. Your character is a dispatch officer for a small police station. Usually, things are quiet. In fact, the most extreme call that has come in is about an elderly resident who once fell but later recovered. Tonight, however, dozens and then hundreds of frantic phone calls come in. A slasher is on the prowl, and the small police force is unequipped to handle it.

46. "Lost but not gone." Dark red messages begin to appear in blood around town, from the sides of restaurants to the driveways of private residences. Understandably, people are creeped out, but they become downright scared when a body shows up and the DNA perfectly matches the blood used in the strange messages.

47. Your character's doorbell rings, and they are surprised to find groceries on their porch. Thinking the delivery driver has messed up the addresses, your character is shocked to see their name on the receipt. That's when they notice someone also wrote three chilling words, "Your last meal."

48. After three teens go missing, your character and others form a search party in the woods surrounding their small town. Somehow, your character veers off course and gets turned around. It is not a body your character finds but the rundown shack in which the slasher has been living.

49. "What is it, boy? Show me!" Your character follows their friendly golden retriever to a patch of disturbed earth in the middle of the community garden. There, your character unearths a bone – a human bone. It seems one of the neighbors has a secret that has now been revealed.

50. The new security vehicle is a welcome relief for residents when it begins to patrol a neighborhood where a string of recent murders occur. Strangely, however, the driver never steps out of the car, and the patrol times curiously match the schedule of recent attacks.

51. "It's called the murder house." Your teen character is told when they point out an abandoned house to their new friends. Immediately, your character wants to know the whole story, and after hearing it, they convince the others to break into the house. Unfortunately for the teens, the murderer is still holed up inside.

52. Imagine a scenario in which a neighborhood kid has begun mowing yards to make extra money for the summer. While cutting someone's house, they happen to witness a murder and are now the target of a slasher's wrath.

53. Angry neighbors fight with each other outside their homes. Someone has been pranking the neighbors, and fingers are pointed out at each other. The real culprit is inside one of the homes, committing a murder while everyone else is outside.

54. Suppose a town's residents wake to find red-stained lawns, their sprinkler systems spurting water tinted like diluted blood. The discovery of strange bones clogging the drains suggests this is no mere plumbing issue.

55. Your character screams in horror as the streetlights illuminate something in the middle of the road – an abandoned stroller splattered with blood. Naturally, your character gets out to check on the poor infant. As it turns out, this is a killer's trap.

56. Suppose a slasher has found the best disguise to get behind the threshold and carry out their evil fantasies against homeowners – a traveling salesman. That is until the salesman picks the *wrong house*, which happens to be the home of a serial killer.

57. Write a horror comedy in which your slasher character has made a grave mistake. They have held a rummage sale and accidentally sold incriminating evidence; whether a murder weapon or an item belonging

to one of their victims. Now they are on a wild goose chase trying to get this back before the neighbor they sold it to notices.

58. The neighborhood's pets go missing, one by one. Naturally, the town is vigilant thinking there is a pet killer on the loose. Thankfully the slasher has left the pets unharmed, but soon, the owners will be as the pets are merely bait for the slayer's misdeeds.

59. "Don't answer the door at midnight." Your character, a house sitter, finds this request rather odd, but of course, they will not argue with the homeowners. That night, someone knocks at the door, precisely at midnight. True to their word, your character does not answer. They then hear someone knocking on the neighbor's door, followed by a blood-curdling scream.

60. Two feuding neighbors constantly accuse each other of crossing property lines. Their wild accusations continue escalating until one is pushed to the edge.

Suppose one becomes a slasher in the making, but not if the other can stop them before the whole neighborhood is in danger.

61. In this horror narrative, write about the rise of a slasher but keep the story within the neighborhood's confines. For example, you can make this more of a horror comedy in which little annoyances push the character to the edge or something more complex, such as a financial loss or the death of a loved one.

62. In the middle of the night, at the small community park, chains on the swing set squeak even though no child is around. Something – or someone – has recently passed through, and in the morning, a fresh body will rest on the merry-go-round for all to see.

63. The neighborhood is one of the most sought-after. It boasts of no traffic, pristine yards, and quiet, simple living. But something breaks through the perfection—a black van circling a specific house, its intentions lethal.

64. Imagine a scenario in which the slasher is trapped in a suburban neighborhood. That is because a scientist has dropped this killer off with robotic victims so that they can conduct their sociological study. Dive into a narrative that questions the ethics of this but also contains lots and lots of bloody fun.

65. Suppose the mail carrier is known for their friendly demeanor and charming personality. The community doesn't realize that the mail carrier has also been dropping off cryptic deliveries with messages that say do not to open until a certain date. When that date finally comes, the killing begins.

66. It's slasher versus slasher in this suburban neighborhood. Suppose two neighbors harbor a dark and ugly secret, but each is unaware that their sinister secret is similar. How do these neighbors find out that they are both killers, and what do they do when they find out?

67. "What's in the attic?" Your character is a house sitter who poses that question to their friend, who has agreed to spend the night with them. Together, the character and their friend brave the attic, even more afraid of the strange creaks and groans across many areas of the house. As it turns out, it isn't the attic they should be worried about. It's the basement.

68. Your character is a dog walker, and one pup is having trouble listening and finally breaks free, darting off into the bushes. Your character follows this dog, not realizing that this pup belongs to the killer, who has purposely commanded their canine to bring their next victim.

69. Imagine a scenario in which property management has given each house in the community the same wind chime as a welcome gift. This gift has an ulterior motive; the collector will claim the quietest homes first.

70. A suburban area does not look the same across the world. Choose a city with a suburb that does not resemble the stereotypical white picket fence setting. Now, create a slash narrative that uses this cultural suburban setting.

Nightmare Campgrounds

Horror set in a remote location is a natural choice for the slasher subgenre. The isolation can create easy suspense, especially when paired with more innocent activities like roasting marshmallows or telling ghost stories by the fire. Whether in a remote cabin or underneath a moonlit lake, these prompts prove that only the wild will hear your screams when you are alone in the woods.

71. Your character is lost in the woods and can't find their way back to the security of the campsite. In the distance, they see a lantern's light and walk toward it, unaware that its owner lures their victims deeper into the woods – never to return.

72. Your character stumbles across a strange shack in the woods. Inside, they discover animal bones, a collection of rusty and bloody tools, and, quite horrifyingly, what looks like a human skull. Then, the door locks and shuts behind them.

73. Campers give each other uneasy glances as they follow the survivalist ahead of them. This person was hired for their wilderness skills and cheaper rate, but now the survivalist directs them deeper into the forest – to their deaths.

74. Your character stumbles across a rotting canoe next to the beach where their group is camping. The interior of the canoe reveals old bloodstains and scratches. Upon closer inspection, the scratches form a message. It reads, "If you are reading this, it's already too late."

75. Imagine a scenario where your character snoops through their bunkmate's backpack. They do not find the valuables they were looking for, but your character does find a series of grotesque photographs that were clearly taken nearby in the woods. If your character says something, not only will they be a target, but their thievery will be found out. What do they do?

76. Your character and their fellow campers are convinced that a wild bear is responsible for a recent death. As they wait for help to arrive, one of the campers realizes the horrifying truth. This is no bear but a slasher that wears the hide of one.

77. "I'm just storing supplies," the camp director says. A few hours later, your character hears, "Off to store some supplies again." After a few days of hearing this, your character finally sneaks into the supply shed. The camp director isn't storing supplies, they're storing bodies.

78. Imagine a scenario in which your slasher character waits for spring showers, knowing the soft ground and heavy rains will silence their footfalls and wash away all traces of evidence. However, before long, no one braves the area in spring or summer anymore. Your character must adapt to the nosey crunch of fall leaves or the crackle of freshly fallen snow. That is if they want to continue to satiate their dark urge.

79. "Nobody is safe in the woods, even you." Your survivalist character is told this by one of the leaders in their mountain training group. Your character brushes it off, knowing that their survival skills are unmatched. Then, their group begins to be picked off, one by one. Does your character feel safe now?

80. Your character thrashes around in the water while they struggle against the chains that bind them. After being tortured for several hours, they have now been left to drown. Will your character free themselves, or will this lake become their tomb?

81. Your character is a slasher stalking someone they think is a mere camper lost in the woods. This is no innocent camper; they are another slasher who wants to expand their territory. Now, it is hunter versus hunter. Who will win?

82. While hiking, your character finds fresh graves amongst the pines. Sufficiently creeped out, your character tries to return to camp, but they completely forget what they just saw once there. That's because the area surrounding these graves is mystical, and the slasher wields both a machete and dark magic.

83. Write a horror narrative that centers on a character who is a silent observer of the comings and goings of a slasher. For instance, suppose this person owns a cabin and watches the slasher pick off teenagers through the window. Why does this person never intervene? Further, why does the slasher seem so indifferent to this character?

84. Imagine a scenario in which your character volunteers at their child's summer camp, hoping to better bond with their child after a recent divorce. Your character and their child will bond all right because it is now up to your character to protect their little one from a slasher.

85. Your character and others wake up in a thicker, darker part of the woods. Somehow, the scene around them looks rather odd – trees have been cut and bunched together, foliage blocks some areas and opens up others, and

there are strange lanterns that light various paths. "It's a maze!" Your character finally exclaims. A slasher has taken them and dumped them inside a maze of their own creation.

86. The strange smell of iron permeates the cabin, waking campers from an otherwise peaceful slumber. Your character is the first to discover the horrifying truth – someone has been shoved into the air conditioner unit, and now their red mist is spraying the area.

87. Your character breaks through a thick part of the forest before diving behind a large, broken tree. Breathing heavily, your character is shocked to see another camper from another campground running scared. Now, your character and this other camper must work together to escape the killer, who is slowly closing in.

88. Rival co-counselors for a luxury camp blame each other for sabotage when supplies vanish, and cabins are vandalized. But as they trade accusations, the real culprit—

watching from the treeline—uses their growing distrust to corner them, one counselor at a time.

89. Every camper who enters cabin 42 has the same terrifying dream – a dark figure scrapes against the cabin door before it breaks open, and the slasher attacks. Finally, your character enters the camp director's office and finds archives, including a camp record that notes cabin 42 as "Condemned After Murders – Opened by Request Only."

90. Your character oversees a huge campground where multiple summer camps co-occur. While patrolling the perimeter, your character finds a small child who claims to have been separated from their group. The hairs rise on the back of your character's head. Something about this child seems off. Surely, this child is not a secret slasher, right? The answer is definitely – yes.

91. An upside-down canoe is the only path to survival for your character. Screams and a slasher's gleeful laughter can be heard outside of it.

Your character just has to hang on a bit longer, but the lake they are in is cold, and if they are not careful, even if they survive the slasher's knife, hypothermia might set in.

92. An old scarecrow has been used for target practice at a summer camp's archery range for years. When pulling out an arrow, your character pulls a little too hard. This reveals a real human skeleton, a murder victim that has finally been found.

93. Write a scenario that deals with the aftermath of a campground slaying. Your character is a detective who has been sent out to investigate the recent slayings, unaware that the killer intends to lead them and the rest of the police force into an already-planned trap.

94. Woodland slashers don't always get a comprehensive backstory; when they do, it's tied to the campground itself. Create a scenario in which even the slasher doesn't know how they got here.

95. Imagine a scenario where two lovers sneak away from the other campers for a secret rendezvous at a nearby cliff. Later, one returns alone, insisting that an "accident" has claimed the life of the other person – though the fresh blood on their hands suggests otherwise.

96. Each spark from the campfire takes on an eerie shape—sometimes resembling silhouettes of fleeing figures. As the gathered campers stare into the flames, they realize these flickers depict the next night's victims, screaming in terror.

97. Your character is an off-duty doctor who has volunteered at the camp infirmary. Your protagonist has expected a few scrapes, bruises, or even a sprain. Instead, multiple victims are carried in, each with a stab wound from a slasher's knife.

98. "Check it out!" Your young character cries as they sit around a campfire with fellow campers. The preteens all oooh and ahhh at the bloody glove your character has found in

the woods, unaware that this belongs to the victim of a nearby slasher.

99. Your character and their best friend are exhausted, hot, and, after a few hours of hiking, even more lost than ever. Their map keeps changing, revealing new paths that lead to even darker places.

100. Write a horror narrative that takes place on a popular beach. During tourist season, a harpoon wielding slasher picks off those who choose to camp at the beach. Now that tourist season has slowed, your character has found it the perfect time to hunt the killer while they lie dormant in the sands.

101. Your character and a group of friends are white water rafting. As the speed picks up and the group careens down the river, your character is certain they witness something in the trees – a bloody body. They have inadvertently spied a slasher's hunting ground.

102. Imagine a scenario in which two groups of campers feud over shared spaces, pranking each other with late-night scares. These pranks are innocent until someone leaves an actual corpse by a bonfire. It seems one of the groups harbors a serial killer who has just awoken.

103. Your character sits on the edge of the dock, admiring their postcard-worthy reflection. Then something disturbs the water, and strange red ripples, followed by a body, crack through the surface.

104. Your character and their partner rent a cabin in the woods for a romantic, intimate weekend. Unbeknownst to either, someone lives in the cellar, eager for the couple's intimate weekend to start.

105. Thus far, your character has survived each trap-laden path and run-in with the masked killer in the woods. Coming to the end of the trail, they find the biggest challenge yet – the killer has brought a friend.

106. A thunderstorm descends on the lakeside cabins, and each thunderclap aligns perfectly with screams across the water. Your

character, who has been out fishing on the lake, now has a dilemma – go back to the cabin and hope these screams aren't people being murdered (they are), or brave the lightning-lit forest and hope there is no additional danger (there is).

107. Write a horror comedy in which your character is the evil slasher in the woods but continues to be thwarted repeatedly by the teenagers they are trying to kill.

108. "If the campfire dies – you run." The small group of campers is told this by their camp leader. They assume this is because of wild animals or because it gets cold in the area. When a rainstorm occurs, and the campfire dies, they learn the truth – a slasher waits in the darkness and uses the lapse in light to attack.

109. "First I heard drumming, then I heard screaming," Your character cries, running a hand along their head bandage as memories bubble to the surface. As your character tells their story inside the camp infirmary, the sound of drumbeats can suddenly be heard from outside of it.

110. Imagine a scenario where your character finds a dog lost in the woods. Of course, your character leans over to pet the canine, immediately wanting to comfort it and bring it to safety. Your character stops because, within the dog's eyes, they see a startling reflection – its master standing behind your character, raising an axe.

111. A flash flood turns the entire camp into a murky swamp, and the heavy rains keep coming. As campers scramble for higher ground, a dark figure in knee-high boots emerges, using the murky water to hide all evidence of their inevitable kills.

112. "But.... she was the strongest swimmer." Your character and others stare at the water where their fellow camper was last seen. Suspicious footprints along the lakeshore end abruptly, as if she walked into the water—and never came out.

113. Picture a scenario where there is not one slasher but dozens. When an infectious disease wipes through the campground, it gives each camper a dose of extreme paranoia. Now, they are stalking each other, wielding whatever weapon they can get their hands on.

114. While hiking, a group of campers discover a strange settlement behind a waterfall. The campers whisper amongst themselves, wondering if the person who lives here is homeless. In reality, nobody lives here, at least not entirely. The slasher camps here to make it easier to sneak out and pick off the campers individually.

115. Your influencer character stumbles across a rusted metal door set into the forest floor while filming content for their social media channel. It takes some effort, but your character finally opens the door and then descends into the darkness. Inside, they find a cramped bunker and newspaper clippings of missing persons from decades ago.

116. A small group of campers head to a secluded clearing at midnight, eager to witness a meteor shower. When the meteors begin to fall, they also illuminate a lone figure in the distance, wielding something that the campers do not see until it's too late.

117. Envision a scenario in which a group of counselors and the campers they oversee have narrowly avoided being murdered. Now, the group is trapped inside a labyrinth underneath the slasher's cabin, and it is up to the counselors to lead the younger kids to safety, even if it means sacrificing themselves.

118. Each camper is assigned a camp duty, and your character now finds themselves crouched over the dock, trying to untangle a collection of rods and lines submerged under the rickety structure. When pulled out, each hook comes up with a necklace, watch, or bracelet from past missing campers.

119. "Everyone must have a buddy!" The rule helps to ensure safety for campers. What happens, however, when that buddy happens to be the slasher?

120. The show must go on! Despite recent disappearances, the annual talent show goes on while investigations by camp leaders continue in the background. In the final act, a camper steps on stage wearing a grotesque costume made of torn camp shirts. The crowd applauds—until they notice the shirt fragments belong to campers who vanished over the last few weeks.

121. A haunting melody can be heard in the woods—someone is humming. The campers are put in a trance and follow the source of the sound, except for one who happens to be wearing headphones. Now, it is up to them to save the others from this mystical musical slasher.

122. For decades, a wooden statue has been erected in the middle of the campground. No one knows its story, but rumors say the statue demands an offering every night - freshly made s'mores, a splash of juice, etc. One year, the campers stop, and a figure

goes looking for a sacrifice that night instead.

123. "Remember, if you see with your flashlight – you will also be seen." Your character is told this before the group explores at night. Campers intend to catch fireflies, watch owls, and find the occasional spider. While the warning is designed for wild animals, as it turns out, it is a lurking slasher the group will have to worry about.

124. Vines snap and your character finds themselves hanging upside down. A figure approaches, an ex-ranger who has been hunting campers who did not heed the warning to stay out of the forest.

125. "Stay calm, I'll lead you back to camp. Over," the camp leader's voice says over the cackling radio. Your character is scared but trusts the voice on the other end. That is – until they see the camp leader's bloody ID badge pinned to a tree with a hunting knife.

126. After lights out, a strange invitation is found on every cabin

pillow. Those who answer are led to a lone campfire burning in a hidden glade. Once everyone is gathered, a menacing figure steps out and says, "Now that you are all here...let the games begin."

127. Someone has been leaving poisoning ivy all around the campground, causing campers to come down with ugly, weeping rashes. This is clearly the work of a slasher, but why? What sinister plans does this slasher have?

128. "The night belongs to me," the slasher growls, wielding a large machete. The campers, who have all had friends die by this person's hands, pull out their own weapons. "Well, now it belongs to us."

129. Each night, a slasher performs a dark ritual that ends with the death of their chosen sacrifice. One camper, who is intended to be the next victim, fights back by ruining the ritual, frustrating the slasher, who feels like they cannot proceed until everything is perfect.

130. Envision a scenario in which a lone deer saves the lives of the remaining campers. How this happens is up to you, whether you want to make this a classic horror or a horror comedy.

131. It is said that if you shout into the gorge, your future will echo back. Of course, most of the time, campers only hear their own words spoken back to them. This time, when a camper tests the myth, the echo comes back in a voice not their own and shouts, "You're next."

132. A group of campers sit by the fire, whispering secrets to each other and giggling long into the night. Little do they know, someone is listening, a stranger who plans to "stumble upon" the campground in the morning. This person will then use the secrets to gain trust, and then – they will slay those who whispered them.

133. Suppose a slasher has a personal vendetta against one specific camper and has no problem leaving the others alone. But the rows of identical tents make it impossible for this killer to find the right one. Do they decide to just go after anyone and everyone, or does this slasher stick to their original plan and continue down the maze of tents until they find their chosen victim?

134. "Why aren't the birds singing anymore?" Your character has been camping with their child, who has asked the question innocently. However, there is nothing innocent about the situation when your character hears the sound of crunching leaves and the telltale sound of a blade opening and closing.

135. While exploring the nearby woods, a group of campers stumble across another abandoned campground. Tents are half-burned, belongings are torn and left behind, and a trail of blood veers off further into the woods. It seems these campers didn't go willingly.

136. A counselor rushes into the camp and screams that a wild animal is prowling the area. Is it a bear? A mountain lion? The counselor is a little vague on the details, but

everyone listens and stays in the camp kitchen as each cabin falls into lockdown. Soon, the real threat becomes clear; the "emergency" is just a ploy for the counselor to trap everyone in the same place.

137. Envision a scenario in which an abandoned summer camp now houses the city's homeless population. When a slasher begins to pick them off one by one, and no one seems to care, this community bands together to protect their own.

138. Your character insists they locked the zipper to their tent right before they went to sleep, but in the morning, they and their partner are shocked to find much of their stuff missing. When your character and their partner exit the tent, they find a trail of their personal belongings, leading them somewhere eerie and mysterious.

139. On the last night of the season, a masked killer takes advantage of the camp tradition – a vigil around the biggest fire yet. However, the campers were expecting this and have been announcing this tradition loud

enough for the slasher to hear, knowing there isn't a vigil. Instead, it is a trap for a killer.

140. Write a horror narrative in which a camp game turns deadly because of a series of strange "accidents." One fellow camper is behind it all.

141. Lanterns dim, crickets go silent, and for one single minute, the campground is bathed in the ghostly light of an eclipse. Within that minute a single scream pierces the air, followed by the hum of the insects and mindless chatter amongst the campers as if nothing ever happened.

142. "Come on, baby. Let's have a little midnight swim." Your character convinces their new love interest to break curfew and eventually go skinny dipping in the nearby lake. The moon's glow illuminates the water, and your character glimpses a shape gliding towards them. It seems they are not alone and certainly not welcome in the slasher's watery domain.

143. Imagine a scenario where your character is always one step behind the killer. Managing to come across each grisly kill is no doubt scary, but it also means your character has just missed the threat. What happens when there is no one else left to slaughter?

144. No one knows who stayed there last, only that one cabin's door is permanently locked from the inside. One stormy evening, the door creaks open, light flickers within, and a sing-song voice calls for unsuspecting visitors.

145. Create a weird horror tale in which the story is told from an unusual source – a squirrel. This squirrel goes about living its rodent life, but what kind of horrors and bloodshed has this creature witnessed?

146. "You stay behind the warding stones, you hear?" Strange ancient rocks form a barrier around this part of the forest. Your character and a few other campers let their thrill-seeking nature take over and cross the barrier later that night. Now, they have awakened a midnight mystic slasher who stalks the area.

Twisted Families & Hidden Ties

Is blood truly thicker than water, or are family ties the cause of more blood? These prompts delve into generational secrets, inherited curses, and long-standing feuds that create strangers with extremely personal killing sprees. When the family legacy turns homicidal, home becomes the last place anyone wants to be.

147. "Our bloodline is cursed for a reason," your character's uncle says, ignoring the pleas to let the victim go. Your character relents but inwardly vows to understand how and why their bloodline is "cursed," using this knowledge to stop the others once and for all.

148. Imagine a scenario in which two siblings have always competed for attention and have even been pitted against each other by various family members. Their aggression has even grown to the point of violence. Then, the siblings find hidden letters and secret diaries that reveal the heart of this rivalry—only one of them will be heir to a grandparent's wealth, and thus, only one is meant to survive.

149. Many prompts will feature biological family ties, but some families are cultivated. Write about a horror "family" built one nomad at a time; people found at rest stops and gas stations and pulled into vans on the side of the road.

150. "That's a nice eulogy, but let me tell you the real story." The funeral is stopped as a family member steps to the podium. They begin divulging disturbing details about the man whose funeral everyone is attending—someone who everyone thought was the pillar of the community—*until today.*

151. Your character finds an old photograph of a family member no one speaks of and is shocked to see the resemblance. The shared likeness is more than a coincidence—it's a prophecy for another murder spree.

152. "Are those.... are those human bones?" Your character asks. They are a painter who has been asked to refresh the nursery but have stopped when they see a mobile fashioned from what looks like tiny bones. The owner of the house smiles and nods, "Oh yes. We never keep the spare."

153. Your character sneaks into an abandoned house, but it isn't abandoned. The family lives in the basement and only surfaces when their next meal goes nosing around the house.

154. Many family-based horror stories deal with a remote area and an improvised clan. Do the opposite for this horror story. An affluent family lives in the middle of the city in one of the only mansions. They use their incredible wealth to make it easy to both catch their victims and cover up their murders.

155. While snooping through their parents' room, your character finds an old family bible. Your character is about to toss it to the side, but then they notice the bloodstains. Opening the book up, they find a list of names in the margins – *victims*.

156. Imagine a scenario that mixes family slashers with the supernatural. A photo album depicts smiling faces that fade over time—except for the background silhouettes that grow clearer. As it turns out, these figures are the original founders of the family, who will soon come back to claim those deemed unworthy.

157. Suppose a sinister family is known as "the eaters," called such because of their cannibalistic tendencies. Of course, this is all just talk from a town that likes to ostracize newcomers. Right? Your character is about to find out the dark truth behind the rumors.

158. The family hunt begins. Each member is supposed to bring one victim, and all guests will be released, screaming, simultaneously. Your character has already told their best friend these sinister plans. Why? Because your character and their best friend are determined to stop this barbaric practice once and for all.

159. A family of influencers has grown in popularity because of their gory, horror content – often showing them killing someone in cold blood. Everyone believes these videos are fake, but before long, viewers realize that they are watching snuff films of actual murders.

160. "Yes, your blood is thick, but theirs is thicker." Your character stares at the knife and backs away. They have been told their blood is too "weak" for the family and now they must join the other victims in the basement. There are also whispers that your character might even be the first sacrifice.

161. Imagine a scenario in which your character always had the same caretaker growing up, who was once the caretaker of their parent. It isn't until your character is a teen that they notice that the caretaker barely ages, and their bedtime stories and whispered lullabies seem...off. Finally, your character discovers the caretaker drinking blood from a vial – the same vial their parents keep on a nightstand.

162. A family is filled with influencers, from makeup gurus to cousins who excel at mukbangs. When one family member becomes more popular than all the others, each family member begins to take it upon themselves to up the ante. This leads to dark and deadly consequences.

163. A rattling chain is heard in the basement at night. Fearful siblings venture downstairs only to find an aunt that everyone was told not to talk about. At first, it is understandable that the siblings would feel sorry for this poor woman, but should they unleash her upon the world, they would understand why she's down there.

164. Attendees arrive at a dinner party expecting forced smiles and awkward small talk but find the mansion's doors locked from the outside. The host announces that this reunion has only one goal: to discover who leaked the family's darkest secret and punish them accordingly.

165. To join a family, your character's fiancé tells them they must make their first kill. Your character is completely shocked, but this is the love of their life, and so they begrudgingly pick up the dagger that bears the family crest. Who do they choose?

166. "Congratulations, sweetie! You are the chosen one," Your character's mother says, holding up satin white robes. Your character immediately begins to sob. They were okay if someone else were chosen to be the next sacrifice, but now that it's them - well, now it's unfair!

167. Write a horror comedy in which a slasher family begins to drift apart when one member refuses to engage in the bloodshed. Finally, the family calls for an intervention. "Remember," the father says, handing this disenfranchised member a knife, "the family that slays together stays together."

168. An arranged marriage has consequences no one expected. One family uses the guise of marriage to find their newest murder victims, not realizing that the other family is planning to do the exact same thing.

169. Your character has finally made it inside the forbidden wing of their family's estate, which has been locked for years. Inside are house paintings of relatives who have met violent ends. Now that your character has entered what they knew was forbidden, their portrait will soon join the others.

170. Your adopted character has just ordered a DNA kit to give them insight into their ancestors. When the results come in, your character is horrified. It seems like they are a descendent of a long line of murderers and serial killers. That begs the age-old question – does evil come by nature or nurture?

171. Every living relative receives the same gilded letter beckoning them to the ancestorial estate for a special celebration. Once there, everyone is seated next to the grand centerpiece, a sealed coffin that bears the guest of honor's name. It seems the patriarch has died, meaning someone in the room must take their place. When weapons are brought into the room, the group realizes it is up to them to decide. Survivor takes all.

172. Write a horror story that takes a family feud to another level when both sets of families try to go after the same victim. While these families are warring with each other, the victim has a chance to get to safety, but will they take this opportunity to survive? Or will they use this distraction to take out each family member individually?

173. "Stay out of the pumpkin patch after dark." A local family is known for their annual pumpkin patch, where neighbors can pick out their favorite. A rebellious teen ignores the sign posted each year and sneaks behind the wooden fence surrounding the giant crop. Once they do, they hear the whir of a chainsaw.

174. Your character has snuck into a neighbor's house, intending to snoop around for valuables. They are hit with an overwhelming smell as soon as they enter the kitchen. It's bodies. Bodies everywhere. Who do these corpses belong to? The family, or are the family themselves killers?

175. Imagine a scenario in which two cousins fall for the same outsider. Their shared obsession turns into a deadly competition, but then, the cousins come to a revelation – why don't they just share? Whether the recipient of their affection is willing or not.

176. Known as the siren, a gorgeous singer becomes the representative of the family, doing everything from renting new leases, going grocery shopping, and, of course, luring unsuspecting victims to their deaths.

177. Your character has grown up in a religious family that condones unspeakable punishments for any offspring deemed "sinful." These punishments are escalating, and the family begins to speak of "purification." In an act of rebellion, your character finds the text the family uses and realizes that purification refers to their next victim's dark and bloody sacrifice.

178. Suppose there is an old homestead that has fallen into disrepair. Eventually, every family member has either died or moved on—except for one. Despite the decay and rot, one family member maintains the land so that they can continue the dark urges that no one is around to stop.

179. Write a horror narrative in which your character is an investigative journalist interviewing a serial killer about their history. The killer begins, "Some murderers are made, but I was born," then proceeds to give a whole backstory of their terrifying family.

180. Your character has been away from the family for years and is no stranger to being called the "prodigal child." When your character returns, each family member is wearing a necklace engraved with their own name, and their greeting is eerily polite—*too polite*. Something is amiss, and your character was right to have left in the first place.

181. Your character is promised a wedding dress by their mother but is told not to look at it before it is altered. Since no photos of said dress are in any family photo album, your character seeks it out. They find it all right, bearing the bloodstains of a previous bride who vanished on her honeymoon.

182. Imagine a scenario in which a family owns an apple orchard that is the talk of the town every Autumn, even though some people who come to pick apples never return.

183. "Each generation must offer one," your character says, staring at their children, grandchildren, great-grandchildren, and great-great-grandchildren. All of which are confused. Then, a sacrificial knife emerges, and everyone is stunned into silence.

184. While rummaging through an antique sewing kit belonging to a grandparent, your character pulls out a pair of ornate scissors covered in blood and gore. Immediately, your character thinks back to local reports of people reportedly stabbed with, you guessed it, scissors.

185. "Don't let them normals see your mark, you hear?" Your young character nods as they head into the elementary school for their very first day. Their parent speaks of the small birthmark that everyone in the family shares, the same mark that the town knows belongs to a family of murderers.

186. Your character runs their hands over the prison glass as their parent does the same on the other end. "Don't worry," your character says in a hushed whisper. "You will be out soon enough." Your character has a plan to break their slasher parent out of prison. Even if it is going to take a lot of dead bodies to do so.

187. Three siblings must work together when they find a diary with coded entries detailing horrific atrocities committed by one of the family members. They want to stop this person but have no idea that this family member is not the only slasher in the clan. In fact, one of the siblings has an even darker secret.

188. Your character has been forced into a family meeting in the dead of night. It seems someone is a snitch and has been talking to the police. Whoever it is isn't going to leave the room alive. A bead of sweat drops down your character's brow. Not only have they been talking, but they are also wearing a wire.

189. "That's why your knife has to stay sharp!" Your character is scolded by an older sibling. Now, the victim has run off with only superficial wounds, and the danger of getting caught is growing.

190. Imagine a scenario in which, instead of birthdays, a slasher family celebrates each member's first kill. How might this be celebrated? Think of what gruesome traditions you can incorporate.

191. Write a horror comedy where your wedding planner is caught in the middle of two murderous families holding a forced reunion to unite their power. Of course, your

character won't be killed (after all, they have a wedding to plan), but they will witness all the bloody shenanigans.

192. Each night, a young child is told a fairytale about a little wolf that is chased away from a colony of rabbits. The wolf grows up to be big and strong before returning to eat all the rabbits. Your character is too young to realize it now, but this story is told as an introduction to the family's true nature.

193. Write from the perspective of someone who is not part of the slasher family but is still involved – the personal assistant. This loyal servant does everything from sharpening weapons to disposing of bodies. This horror story should be more of a day-in-the-life style narrative of this assistant.

194. Your character is a small-town doctor sent to help a remote family that most people try to avoid. Once your character arrives, the murderous family demands they save their patriarch; otherwise, your

character will get the same treatment as their victims.

195. "Everyone must earn their mask, and you are no different." Your character knows they must make one more kill before getting a mask bestowed by their family. Write a story showcasing your character's last kill and what mask and name they will be given.

196. Write a scenario in which siblings compete in a new sport – the body count of hitchhikers that pass by their remote property. All of this changes, however, when one sibling falls in love with the next intended victim.

197. "You know boys are only after one thing," a mother says to a teenage daughter who has just started dating. "And that is the very thing that will give you what you want." The mother smiles wickedly and continues, "An easy kill."

198. Suppose there is a slasher family that speaks their own unique language. One day, your character is out walking in the woods when they

suddenly hear a foreign tongue shouting about their arrival.

199. "Why are there so many empty chairs?" Some forks clatter as soon as the words are spoken, while others hang in mid-air. The visiting cousin who has just spoken gulps as dark tension hangs in silence. "They tried to leave," someone finally says, "So, don't you get the same idea."

200. Your character is given a giant box for their birthday by a family member, and when they open it, they find a victim bound and gagged. Is your character happy about this "gift," or are they revolted?

201. Each family member must conduct a fresh kill by midnight to secure their spot in a will. Consider the perspectives of each of these family members, both their success and their triumphs.

202. Many times, a slasher family sticks together. In this scenario, suppose one family member left because of how horrible the family treated them. Years later, this very character has returned, and that's when bloody revenge begins.

203. Neighbors accept an offer to dine at the mansion, expecting polite conversation and roast beef. Instead, the main dish is delivered by the eerie matriarch who brandishes a cleaver with unsettling finesse—and a glint of hunger in her eyes.

204. For a slasher family, an annual reunion has many elements of a non-slasher family's – there's music, good food, and plenty of decorations. What is different is what everyone is wearing – a mask signifying how many lives they've claimed. What does your character's mask look like?

205. Dummies carefully hand-stitched from bits of dried skin, bone, and fabric sit stoically at the family dinner table. This ensures that the "ancestors" can watch all future generations continue participating in each nightly slaughter.

206. Each dawn, the household raises a glass of what appears to be wine in

solemn unison. An unsuspecting guest who sneaks a taste realizes it's warm and metallic, and now the family insists that they are "a part of the clan" in more ways than one.

207. Family weddings, baptisms, and funerals are held at a barn at the back of the property. Your character, a journalist, has been studying the family for quite some time and has managed to sneak into the barn during one such event. Little do they know, the family is aware of their snooping, and this celebration will be the annual sacrifice.

208. Instead of Secret Santa, this slasher family participates in "secret slaying." Every member of the family must bring a victim for someone else.

209. When your character is taken by a murderous cult family that worships a strange deity, they think of an ingenious way to survive – pretend to be the deity reincarnated in human form.

210. Photographs, bloody garments, and strings of teeth hang from the ceiling as souvenirs of every victim. When your adopted character stumbles across this disturbing collection in their new family's home, they are told they will add to it one day.

211. On the eve of their eighteenth birthday, each child receives a black envelope naming who they must kill to maintain the family fortune. Everyone gets names of people who have harmed the family somehow – judges, social workers, etc. Except for one. A cousin draws your character's name.

212. "Stay away from the third floor. Otherwise, you can go wherever you want." After their parents die in an accident, your character is taken in by a foster family. This rule seems simple until curiosity gets the best of your character one night, and they enter the third floor. That's when your character finds startling evidence that their parents' deaths weren't an accident at all. It was murder.

213. One of the most interesting tropes in horror is how a slasher family kills with impunity, and the bodies always seem to be piling up despite the likelihood that they would eventually be caught, or someone would fight back with lethal force. Write a story that deals with a more realistic take on this scenario.

214. "Don't you see, I only wanted to protect you," your character stares up at their slasher parent and then the dead body that lies behind them. Is this true? Or is this just an excuse for a murder their parent was going to commit anyway?

215. A family gathers at the main estate to read the will, but rather than sharing who will inherit what, the will reveals treacherous secrets and hidden alliances. Now that everyone's dirty laundry is out, the real question is, who will inherit the knife.

Fanatics & Deadly Devotions

What happens when a horror killer has a motive that goes deeper than bloodlust? Very, very bad things tend to happen. These writing prompts deal with slasher zealots driven by religious fervor, political desire, or another ideology. These fanatical foes believe that every victim is a necessary sacrifice for a higher cause.

216. "The congregation must be cleansed," a charismatic leader says to their second in command, who protests. That reluctance is soon halted when blood begins to spill.

217. Suppose there is a fiery prophet who believes the apocalypse is coming through fire and brimstone. Rather than wait for it to happen, however, this so-called prophet travels from town to town, setting homes ablaze. When townspeople naturally run out screaming, they will find the prophet standing calming—one hand holds a torch and the other a blade.

218. "Sign the pledge or face the blade." Your character frowns at the contract held before them. Behind the speaker lies a pile of bodies stacked on each other. Does your character sign in blood? Or do they resist and face the blade?

219. Create a scenario that prominently features an alphabet killer. You can decide whether this person targets those with the same letter of the alphabet (e.g., A is for Ana, B is for Benny, etc.) or the kill is inspired by a letter of the alphabet (e.g., A is for asphyxiation, b is for bashing, etc.). No matter what you decide, you must also come up with why this character is motivated towards this unique slaying style.

220. When a family member is denied insurance coverage for a life-saving operation, your character swears revenge after their relative's preventable death. What form does this take? Towards those involved in the insurance case, the medical team that your character feels "did not do enough," or another group entirely?

221. An animal rights group takes activities to the extreme when they begin to hunt humans in the same way that animals are hunted. Your character, a former member, is the only one who might be able to get them to see reason.

222. "I am a self-appointed angel," The slasher declares, spreading their arms wide towards the heavens. Your character has been listening to this person's rants from their "book of Ascension" for almost four hours. Thus far, your character has managed to avoid the blade, but time is running out.

223. A polygamy cult has been in decline for quite some time, and numbers are fading to the point where the cult might disappear entirely in a generation or two. Your character has been tasked with finding more people to boost the numbers, even using force if necessary. It seems your character is taking that last direction a little too seriously because, so far, everyone they recruit has "accidentally" been killed.

224. Certain that a tragic accident involving their child is caused by a specific political group, a grieving parent becomes a slasher that targets leaders of this movement. To be sure your character's message is loud and clear, they also leave behind pamphlets calling for continued bloodshed.

225. A traveling minister sets up a makeshift confessional at carnivals, luring the lost and the guilty. When victims are too plentiful, some even willing to become the next sacrifice, the minister becomes bored. How does this religious slasher decide to up the ante?

226. Imagine a scenario in which a spiritual guru holds a popular luxury retreat high in the mountains, even though nobody is ever changed for the better. This is the sole reason your character, who happens to be a slasher who goes after such charlatan types, has booked a stay.

227. "Blessed are the meek, for they shall inherit my sword." This phrase, written in blood, has started to show up across the city – graffiti on billboards, etched on park benches, and even on the sidewalk outside the police station. While everyone else fearfully stays behind locked houses to escape the killer, your character has decided to figure out what this phrase means so they can go after the slasher themselves.

228. A cult believes that an alien is supposed to take over the body of the leader, and then everyone is meant to go to a distant planet together. Now suppose a slasher has learned of this cult and believes this group will be easy prey. After all, they only need to convince this group that they are this so-called leader. Little does this slasher realize that the group is quick to see through the ruse and has sinister plans for this slasher.

229. A protester turns into a violent slasher, targeting the city's elite in brutal nighttime slayings. Each victim receives a blood-smeared manifesto decrying economic inequality—a final warning that no fortune can buy safety.

230. Many motivations featured in this prompt section have a specific political, social, or religious goal. Instead, craft a scenario in which a slasher is an extreme conspiracy theorist, believing

anything and everything to justify their kills.

231. "I tried to enlighten you, but you wouldn't listen!" Your character is on the receiving end of these words, spoken by a former best friend. This friend has been trying to convince your character of their misguided and deadly beliefs for years. Your character refused to give in, and now, the deadly consequences have arrived.

232. "There will be no more broken judicial systems on my watch," a character growls as they attack. This character is a former public defender who becomes convinced justice can no longer be achieved in court. Now, they attack the criminals they are certain will walk free, but are they not a criminal themselves with this twisted interpretation of law and order?

233. A group of students begin meeting after school for a social club. With no teacher oversight, the group sets the meeting agenda, which usually involves truth or dare. However, these meetings continue to escalate to the point of ritualistic murder.

234. Your character is a super fan of a TV show, from attending fan events in cosplay to roleplaying on private message boards. Everything about their life becomes like this show. Then the show gets canceled after five seasons. What happens next? Does your character decide to take out the network responsible, or do they pick up the mantle of one of their favorite characters, even if it means certain death of hapless victims to recreate new scenes?

235. Envision a scenario in which a character has a break in reality between the waking world and the RPG they are obsessed with roleplaying. So much so that they become exactly like their slasher character.

236. "They will never EVER censor me again." Suppose a disgraced social media influencer vows revenge on the many platforms that silenced them. Now, each new kill is live-streamed to a secret channel, transforming this character's personal grudge into a viral, nightmarish spectacle.

237. A small island becomes the newest vacation destination, but the people who have been native to these islands for thousands of years are not happy about the outsiders who destroy the once serene beach with trash, overfish, or bring hatred towards the native population. Your character vows to stop them, even if every last tourist must die for others to get the message.

238. Your character does not consider themselves a slasher because they leave their victims alive and "better off." They do this by targeting people with "toxic habits," such as smokers and food addicts. Your character then substitutes these habits with lethal injections, and to survive, these people merely must take it upon themselves to "get help and recover."

239. "Protect the unborn!" Your character watches the protesters closely, like a predator to prey. They choose one, perhaps the most opinionated and judgemental, and then follow their new victim home. As it turns out, your character was a child who grew with countless abusive foster families. Do they only target the protesters, and if so, what happens if they are found out?

240. Your character hears someone outside their apartment, and when they check, they find their suspicions are correct. Someone has taped a rambling letter to their door, accusing your character of being part of a secret government cabal. How can they clear up this confusion before they become this slasher's next victim?

241. An eco-activist takes the next step when their latest protest, a sit-in in front of an oil company, is met with deaf ears. This character turns into a slasher, first targeting industrial workers. When these murders prove to be "too easy," the eco-slasher targets big-business CEOs, and finally, they get the attention they want.

242. Your character is a politician who has taken to eliminating the opposing campaign staff individually. Thus far, your character has gotten away with it. Then, there is a single bloody ballot that ties them to the latest murder.

243. Envision a scenario in which a slasher does not think themselves a ruthless killer, even though they are. Instead, this character believes that they are absorbing the sins of others through the act of murder and, thus, are making themselves purer in doing so.

244. A slasher releases toxic chemicals inside an office building, wearing their trademark gas mask. Why? Because this company is responsible for millions of gallons of toxic waste dumped in rivers across the country. This building is just one of many this slasher plans to target.

245. A small group stands together in the woods solemnly and in silence. Surrounding them are thick trees that have stood for thousands of years. And on those trees? Bodies of victims, all of which have been murdered by this strange cult.

246. Your character has been working at the same company for nearly a decade before they are fired after asking to take medical leave. Your character cannot afford to fight this wrongful termination in court and instead chooses to get revenge one manager at a time.

247. Imagine a scenario in which a slasher cult leader forces followers to air every secret they hold in a nightly gathering. "Confess your desires or die." Your character has decided there is a third option – *kill and take over*.

248. A two-party political system is never good, especially when both sides have retained a notorious slasher to take out cabinet members on the other side. What happens when these two assassins work together to abolish the government?

249. A group of cult followers trudge after a charismatic leader in a single-file line across the desert. This pilgrimage will not lead to enlightenment like the group is told, but certain death.

250. After receiving a diagnosis of a rare brain tumor, your character's personality shifts completely, and now, they have decided that a creature named "Grik" has commanded them to kill. Everyone is convinced that it is the disease ravaging your character's mind, but what if Grik is not only real but they are a sentient anomaly that sits in your character's brain.

251. Imagine a scenario where a group of zealots work together to remove the "unworthy souls" in their community. How does your character know these fanatical slashers have targeted them next? Because of the cryptic verses that were hacked in their door overnight.

252. Your slasher character is convinced divine justice requires a human touch. While this typically might mean laying hands on someone in prayer, for your character, it means branding the "sinful" with a cross before chasing them with a dagger in the dead of night.

253. Your character seems aloof and apathetic at the high school reunion, much like they did back in school. That's precisely what your character wants – to fade into the background so that they can pick off those who bullied them, one by one.

254. After submitting their resumes to thousands of companies and making it to the third, fourth, and sometimes even fifth round of interviews, your character has yet to find a job. Now, it is your character who will "interview" past recruiters and hiring managers alike. Those who are chosen will be a given a job – of survival.

255. From the ashes of a cult that took their own lives rises a slasher who is intent on carrying on the message that others have died for. If previous members are now gone, what ties to deceased cult members might this slasher's victims have?

256. Write a scenario where a slasher uses social engineering to lead their victims to the same shady hotel room. The slasher does this through social media, message boards, and emails. How long will it be until this slasher is caught? That is, if they ever are.

257. Suppose there is an anti-gentrification slasher that only targets real estate developers, and after each slaying, they leave eviction notices on the high rises each victim owned. Unfortunately, these slayings have the opposite effect that the slasher wanted, and property values skyrocket as the wealthy want to "reclaim the streets."

258. Write a horror comedy in which a knitting club seems unassuming on the outside, comprised primarily of the elderly. The group creates woven pieces for children's hospital wards, elderly folks' homes, and pet shelters. However, this club hides a sinister secret – a recruit must bring in a sacrifice, for the group believes that their power to crotchet and knit comes straight from the devil.

259. "Those who destroy the forest must be the ones who regrow it." A reclusive arborist cultivates a secret orchard of twisted trees grown from human remains. At night, each new victim is dragged into the orchard, their fate marked by a freshly dug pit and a single, ominous sapling.

260. Blend a touch of mysticism with the zealot slasher narrative. After a church burns down with a priest inside, they are reborn as a disfigured stranger who have been gifted with strange mystic powers, which they use to seek out and kill the sinful.

261. "Just one last story, that's all I need," your journalist character says, but this is untrue. Your character is disgraced in the journalism world, and these sit-downs, driven under the guise of a groundbreaking exposé, always end the same – with a slash from a blade that ensures these secrets die with the interviewee.

262. Known as the New Zodiac Slayer, a slasher armed with an astrolabe and carrying ceremonial daggers marks each murder scene with the victim's astrological chart. Create a

backstory as to why this killer takes this strange approach to their slayings.

263. "Don't worry about the taste. This will be your final meal, after all." A chef targets food critics and trendy gourmets, having had their own classic dishes rejected as palates change. Victims find themselves force-fed bizarre concoctions in underground kitchens, ending with the chef's knife carving their personal signature into the final dish.

264. A famous cosplayer has had enough of people who claim to be true fans invading fandom culture. As a result, this cosplayer stalks conventions for these so-called fake fans, killing victims in ways that are reminiscent of their favorite scenes from comics and movies. Catching them will be hard because different "characters" are behind the crimes.

265. This slasher is known by many names—the trash collector, the sewer rat, and the garbage menace. Those names don't do justice to the intricate planning the slasher does, from understanding the city's interworking to slinking in and out of drainage pipes.

266. A slasher takes content moderation to the real world when they begin to track down and kill cyberbullies and online trolls. Each gruesome kill has a placard next to the body that reads, "Removed for Violating Community Guidelines."

267. Envision a character who is a true "mother-in-law" from hell. Determined to rid her child of any unsuitable partners, this slasher orchestrates fatal "accidents" for would-be fiancés. Finally, a suitable candidate is found, but in an ironic twist, this is another slasher with their own dark secrets.

268. A librarian has been a slasher for decades, using victims for a new type of collection tucked away underneath the building where the library stands. Your character and a friend will be the first to discover their horrific shrine.

269. According to the policy paper laid next to each victim's body, a slasher believes these deaths will lead to political reform. After decades, the slasher becomes disappointed when nothing ever comes from it. As a result, the slasher decides to launch their own political campaign, openly admitting to what they have done.

270. A former child star blames the entire industry for their downward spiral. Now, this former star hunts current celebrities, whispering, "It's time to end your fame," before committing each murder.

271. An embittered online personality turns "cancel culture" into a real-life campaign of vengeance. Each target is found bearing a hashtag carved into their skin, and if one were to look it up, they would find similar victims, all grotesquely posed and contributing to the overall message of revenge.

272. A manifesto is pinned to the door of city hall, but no one takes it seriously. Then, every building in the city has rigged stairwells, elevators, and escalators, all of which become death traps for unsuspecting townspeople. What exactly was in that manifesto?

273. "It's not my fault. The future speaks, and I listen." Suppose a tarot card reader believes each card pulled indicates who might die. To ensure their prophecy is correct, the tarot card reader aligns destinies perfectly with their blade.

274. A slasher carries around a stone tablet, believing they are Moses reincarnated in human form. They say they want to take certain people to the promised land through sharpened staff. What is the promised land, and who is chosen?

275. What is worse than a slasher? Perhaps a slasher with a military background. In this scenario, an ex-military officer is determined to eliminate those who have turned their backs on the country. The problem is that the phone lines and text messages this slasher has intercepted only tell half the

story, and their assumptions have already cost countless lives.

276. Create a horror narrative only through texts, emails, and social media messages. That is because the slasher is a data miner who lures unsuspecting victims into terrible situations, which they orchestrate. Consider whether this is true "murder" since the victims suffer accidents or take their own lives, and if so, by what degree?

277. An eco-friendly slasher believes that city dwellers are corrupting the natural order. Thus, they lure tourists to a remote rural area, promising a complete farm-to-table experience. They fail to mention that these tourists are intended to be the livestock, and their screams will be silenced by the hum of barn machinery.

278. Suppose a person hates avarice so much that they become a slasher, vowing to go after the affluent and extremely wealthy. However, to do so, it will take funds to get into places where only the elite are allowed to go. What happens when this slasher character becomes what they hate?

279. Masks, veils, and confetti are all part of a slasher's grisly tableau. No one quite knows why this killer targets wedding ceremonies, only that afterward, one partner is left unharmed, and the other is the main attraction in the grisly display.

280. Write a scenario in which a doomsday prepper becomes a slasher when they are convinced the world's end is near. Their hideout is lined with tinned food, scribbled plans, and a series of personal belongings, the latter of which came from the victims taken from grocery stores and gas stations.

281. Suppose grieving parents have two unique coping methods after all their children die in a terrible accident. The first stalks playgrounds and suburban homes, choosing who they deem as "unfit parents" for their victims. The other parent tries to stop the new slasher in town.

282. "Cheaters never win" is the last thing a cheating partner hears before they become a victim of the jilted lover slayer.

283. Within a desolate warehouse, deep within the forest, a slasher forces their victim to hear a hand-written manifesto at knifepoint. This slasher is going to kill each victim either way, but they want to be sure each one understands their reasoning. What exactly is that reason?

284. The small town in which your character lives is surrounded by mountains of clothes, dumped there because of the fast fashion industrial giants overseas. Your character has plans to travel to this land and murder those responsible for this fabric plague. Soon, that dream becomes a reality.

285. Write a horror narrative that also blends in social commentary. A slasher, who is heavily invested in genealogy, is convinced that certain bloodlines weaken society, and they further believe that it is their sole duty to kill them off.

286. Your character is convinced that AI will eventually erase and replace humanity. Armed with stolen prototypes, they target IT magnates, CEOs, and others who seek to "usher in the digital apocalypse."

287. "My art is my everything," a slasher whispers as they take the life of yet another victim. After failing as an artist and even being ostracized from the creative community, the slasher decides to hold their own gallery showing, with all the victims arranged in one elaborate and chilling crime scene.

288. Envision a scenario where a slasher is also an accomplished hacker who targets corporate moguls. Using blackmail, the slasher convinces these affluent people to meet them at secluded spots, where, one by one, they are later found dead with file folders full of those same secrets placed on top of them.

289. Think of a slasher motivation that has not been featured in this prompt book. Craft a character with this motivation but create a twist – this character must realize that their cause is unjustified and vows to stop. It's too late, however, because a family member of a previous victim has promised to kill them in kind.

Urban Legends Come Alive

Told in hushed voices at sleepovers or shared through email chains, urban legends have a way of wrapping their sinister fists around the throats of every generation. These prompts deal with modern folklore, showing that there is a thin line between shared myth and disturbing reality.

290. A fateful road sign has been marked with graffiti, repainted, and then marked again. The graffiti is always the same—*those who travel never return*. Dive into the story of the slasher who caused the need for this graffiti and who is responsible for trying to warn others.

291. A town is under siege when a mysterious number floods the local area with weird, cryptic voicemails that begin with static and end with

faint breathing. It is said that those who listen too closely hear their own names whispered, and if they stay on the line, eventually, someone will knock at the door.

292. After watching a certain clown horror film, a group of kids warn each other about staying away from the storm drain. They are convinced that a pale hand will reach out each time it rains. Of course, movies aren't real, are they? Not quite. It isn't a clown the children should be worried about, but a very human and very threatening murderer who lives amongst the sewage.

293. Imagine an urban legend surrounding a traveling thrift store merchant. This "oddities & ends" merchant is said to appear at random pop-up markets, offering the most unusual and rare finds through unbeatable deals. Although the items are one-of-a-kind, they are also torn and slightly stained, and anyone who brings them home swears they are haunted. The merchant is always a little cagey about where they got said items.

294. At 2 am every night, residents in a single suburb hear a strange, drawn-out whistle echoing through the streets. Known as the "night whistle," those who whistle back are said to disappear by morning.

295. A popular video aggregator website generates buzz when an account is reported, then banned, and then appears with the same viewer and subscriber count moments later. The videos all show the same thing—the final moments of those who vanished without explanation. Stranger still, investigations uncover no record of the uploader.

296. At an abandoned playground, adults who remember playing in the area when they were little whisper to each other about the swing that moves even when no wind blows. When the first body appears, the adults realize that they are not delusional; someone is stalking the area, even though the last child grew up decades ago.

297. Write a horror comedy that involves a neon billboard featuring a disco ball, a glitter mascot, and a countdown. Local rumors say that the radio will fill with screams if you drive by when the countdown hits the final minute. Then, HE will appear in the backseat.

298. Chain emails were prominent in the early 2000s. They often warned, "Pass this on to 20 people, or someone you love will die." This was before social media or widely available fact-checking websites, so naturally, people believed them without a second thought. Create your own spin on the idea of a chain email, creating a slasher that will attack those who do not keep the chain going.

299. Suppose a city subway has an urban legend surrounding one of the cars. "Take the third subway car at your own risk." It is said that multiple people have died there, and if one peers in, it really does look like both fresh blood line the walls and booths. When your character is late for an appointment, they have no choice but to take the empty car. Once they do, the subway car's lights flicker and turn off completely.

300. On a busy highway, motorists see an advertisement that appears blank, at least to some. For others, it is reported that this same billboard depicts disturbing, graphic images of grisly deaths. Why is it that some of the population sees these images, and further, what kind of slasher is behind the barbaric display?

301. Create an urban legend that involves a killer clown that haunts theme parks, carnivals, and local pizza parlors. They lure their victims by leaving tarnished tokens, and the children cashing in are immediately marked. Your character, a child who was able to get away, has returned to the small town where this has happened, determined to save others from a terrible fate.

302. On the edge of town, there is a crumbling building near the riverside that is half submerged. Under the full moon, the building can barely be seen. There are whispers of ghosts surrounding its halls and speculation of what the building might have once been. Your character and a friend finally sneak inside. With horror, they realize that this building was once an asylum and a slasher waits inside, having never left.

303. Envision a scenario in which a vintage taxi appears one morning, picks up a rider, and then spends the entire day meandering along the highway, destination unknown. Naturally, one would assume that this taxi driver is the slasher, wasting time and frustrating their passengers with the knowledge of something amiss. It is actually the passenger who is the killer of legends, and the driver is trying to bide time to save their own life.

304. Your character and friends have snuck out of the house. There is a legend of a local record store that is only open at night and in a secret location. The store is said to sell vinyl records that allegedly capture the final moments of the missing. Your character and their friends manage to find the store, but they find out too late how those screams are captured.

305. Your character chats with who they think is their best friend on Messenger. It isn't. They are chatting with a stranger with a similar screenname, which is all by design. The slasher uses shared secrets to isolate their victims, and then, when they are most vulnerable, the slasher attacks.

306. Write a horror comedy that takes place in a high school. There is a rumor that the last stall in the boy's bathroom contains more than just grossness. Instead, there is supposed to be a slasher that lives in the toilet and will kill any student who sits too long. Your character sets a camera determined to catch this slasher in the action.

307. Think of a popular nursery rhyme, perhaps even one you grew up with as a child. Now, create an urban legend slasher who uses this little tune to lure out their would-be victims.

308. Your character has constant nightmares of falling down an elevator shaft. One day, they are casually mentioning it to a coworker

who then relates an urban legend they heard – a slasher pushes victims into an elevator shaft. Not high enough to kill them, but high enough to keep them from running away. Later, when your character takes their usual elevator, there is a strange draft, and suddenly your character is pushed into the darkness.

309. Suppose there is an alleyway that people try to avoid at all costs. Why? It is said that there is a "haunted wall" that hums, scratches, and occasionally even screams. The other side of this wall is a standard store shelf that is part of a small grocer. Does the wall contain the cries of past victims? Is someone stuck in the wall, or is this just a sinister way for an urban legend slasher to lure their victims?

310. Considered one of the last pay phones in a large city, it rings continuously at midnight. No one dares answer it save for your character. There is a lone cry for help, static, and then the phone rings again. This time, another voice cries for help. Your character doesn't know it yet, but they are listening to the cries of slasher victims.

311. A group of mall employees whisper to each other about a hunched creature that lives in the crawlspace beneath the escalators. In fact, even customers report feeling a tug on their shoelaces, while others report seeing eyes staring up from small cracks. It isn't a monster, though; it's a slasher.

312. Write the story of a young slasher, a child who themselves were slain and are still searching for the address where it happened. It is said that if someone answers the door at exactly 2:17 am (precisely the moment this child died), the homeowner will be met with the same brutal end.

313. Your character has a tooth in serious need of pulling. Not having much money, your character finds an ad in the paper that promises free dental procedures in exchange for a 5-star review. When your character discovers the office is in an abandoned mall, they are hesitant. They are right to be wary; this dentist collects more than teeth but also collects lives.

314. "He will knock on the door three times. If you don't let him in, you don't want that fourth knock." Create a story that involves an urban legend surrounding a mail carrier who died decades ago. Those who let this figure in will get a letter from a lost loved one. Those who wait for the fourth knock are said to be taken out in pieces, carried by mailbag.

315. Suppose there is a secret paranormal club that meets after hours at a local library. Attendees share ghost stories and urban legends, eat plenty of snacks, and drink lots of coffee. One night, someone sees a shadow moving between the shelves. It seems a slasher exists, and they have decided to bring the group's tall tales to life.

316. "You should always leave one earbud out when you run. Otherwise, you won't hear someone else's footsteps." Your character is warned

this by a parent, again and again. Of course, your character doesn't listen. Until the music skips, and through both earbuds, they hear an additional pair of footsteps just behind them, followed by heavy breathing.

317. Deserted gas stations, or even those in remote locations, are prominent in urban legends. Create a horror story in which this gas station doesn't set the stage for a local legend slasher but offers sanctuary from one.

318. Passengers in the backseat of a mid-sized SUV cast worried glances at each other. The rideshare driver has not spoken and is unsettlingly still. One of the passengers then notices that the app wasn't tracing the trip's start and end point while another is startled to find there are no car door handles.

319. Spray-painted messages appear on multiple abandoned buildings, referencing tomorrow's date and an unknown name. By dawn, each message changes to an obituary note describing a bizarre death that

perfectly fits the name scrawled the night before.

320. Imagine a scenario in which a strange Wi-Fi network appears on cell phones in remote places, even those isolated for hundreds of miles. When someone connects, their phone begins to beep, and they realize too late that it is now a tracking device.

321. *Warning! Do Not Use This Vending Machine.* At first, your character heeds the warning, not wanting to lose their money, but curiosity gets the best of them. After all, what if the vending machine spits out two candy bars instead of one? After trying it, the vending machine dispenses more than extra candy bars. It also spits out old photographs, children's toys, and even small bones. It's almost as if the vending machine holds a serial killer's secret stash.

322. Write a horror comedy in which your character and friends summon a slasher in random location using an old Ouija board. The more well-known

the location and absurd the story, the better.

323. There are many tales of "lost media," which are visual, audio, or audiovisual files like music or films that are either irretrievable or lost to the public. Create your own form of lost media associated with a unique slasher.

324. "If you see a stranger in your reflection, don't turn off the lights." A viral social media challenge dares participants to stare at the mirror at midnight. Each video always ends with this ominous warning. For most participants, nothing happens, but for your character, the reflection distorts, and when they turn off the lights, the dark figure appears.

325. "What's wrong with this stupid thing!" Your character ejects the tape, not realizing they eject the slasher with it. For this scenario, include a movie rental store and at least one disgruntled employee. You can decide if this is a horror comedy or a classic fear fest.

326. Suppose there was a horrific accident years ago when a little boy got stuck and then crushed in a trash compactor. Locals say that if you go to this specific dumpster, still next to the elementary, and say "Dirty Danny" three times, you will be dragged in with him.

327. In Korea and other Asian countries, there is an urban legend known as "The Elevator Game." Meant to be played alone, and in a building with at least 10 floors, one must go to ascending or descending floors in a specific order. For example, go to the 4th floor and then the 2nd floor. The goal is to see an otherworldly woman and eventually go "elsewhere." In your version, the game ends with a slasher taking their next victim.

328. The Hook-Man legend goes like this: Two sweethearts park on Lover's Lane after hearing about a killer in the area. The car radio crackles with metallic static, and a scrape echoes across the door. The story ends in different ways, but usually with the couple dead and a hook embedded in the roof of the car. Create a similar horror story, but this time, suppose the couple are the slashers. Now, the Hook-Man will be the one who struggles to get away.

329. Write a story about Kuchisake-Onna and her terrible scissors. In this scenario, a strange woman randomly appears in a bustling Tokyo suburb wearing a surgical mask. "Am I pretty?" she asks before branding oversized shears, intent on cutting those who dare to meet her gaze.

330. Many urban legend slasher stories were created around the 1970s to 1980s because of the many abandoned insane asylums that closed a decade earlier, such as Staten Island's Cropsey. Research a few of these abandoned places and create your own slasher but elevate the story by integrating social commentary.

331. Your character and friends sit underneath a bridge, expecting the infamous Bunny Man to appear. Sure enough, a man dressed in a ragged and bloodstained rabbit costume shows up. His hatchet glints under the moonlight, but your teen character and their friends were expecting this and pull out the wooden bats hidden behind their backs.

332. A group of students tease a new classmate about the three cute baby animal stickers on their binder. This newcomer ignores the taunts, and the next day, it is reported that someone in the classroom has gone missing. With a knowing grin, the new student adds another sticker to the collection.

333. Your character is a detective called to investigate a series of strange deaths on the highway. No one could prepare your character for what they are about to see – stranded cars stretched across twenty miles filled with drivers who have met the sharpened end of a crowbar. It seems the hitchhiker slasher has struck again.

334. Your character is being stalked by a slasher. Not just any, but your character is convinced it is a Venezuelan killer known as *El Silbón*, which translates to the whistler. How does your character know this slasher has been stalking them? Because each time they go outside, especially at night, someone whistles threateningly.

335. Legend speaks of the Bandage Man of Cannon Beach, a mutilated figure who roams coastal highways draped in bandages. Now, drivers claim he leaps onto their cars, leaving bloody gauze in his wake. The absolute terror in story is that he's no ghost, just an angry slasher whose burning rage fuels him to shred unsuspecting travelers who venture too close to the dunes at night.

336. Write a horror from the perspective of a child who fears the "treacherous toilet" and refuses to potty train. The story should involve the parents' frustration and how this inadvertently will cause a slasher to be found and caught. How? That's entirely up to you!

337. Inspired by clown sightings, an ex-entertainer seeks vengeance on those who mock their profession. This killer clown lures people with promises of a "private show," and if they agree, these hapless victims will soon find themselves with a permanent grin.

338. Truckers talk of Slaughterhouse Sam, a butcher who died in a fiery crash and supposedly roams Route 66. But Sam is alive—a vengeful mechanic wearing a scorched leather apron, capturing late-night travelers. Each morning, battered trucks are found with "Sam Was Here" carved into metal, the drivers nowhere in sight.

339. Your character is walking home late at night in an area they have never been in before. They soon come to a crossroads. It doesn't matter which choice they take because your character will find an urban legend slasher at either end.

340. For decades, kids have warned each other about alligators flushed in the toilet as babies, only to grow up to become full-grown people-eating gators. The same is true of pythons and, of course, rats. Tell an even scarier story in which people vanish near commodes and manhole covers, all the result of the "Sewer Slayer" who uses these

abandoned pets for their own nefarious misdeeds.

341. "You're not a ghost, are you?" Your character jokes, looking at the woman wearing a wedding dress in the backseat of their car. Your character has heard of the fake hitchhiker bride urban legend, in which a Good Samaritan picks up a ghost. But this bride is no ghost – she's a slasher.

342. The secret slasher has been responsible for several deaths thus far, and the townsfolk are convinced this is the work of an urban legend come to life. But the two are unrelated. Now, the killer behind the urban legend has decided to get involved—upset that they are getting the credit for someone else's "sloppy handiwork."

343. At one of the most famous theme parks on Earth, it is said a decommissioned mascot roams the park after hours, killing anyone who lingers. Over time, park security ramps up, and the legend dies down. That is until your characters and a group of friends hide until the park is closed. That's when they hear a familiar jingle – a famous song, and a fuzzy figure coming closer.

344. Joggers report seeing a rickety bicycle leaning against the railing of a dimly lit bridge. When they slow down to look, they spot muddy footprints leading into the woods—and the glint of a blade from an urban legend slasher who lures those who stop to help.

345. Local legend says a faceless fiend abducts children, and your character, a new parent, is determined to be extra vigilant. They recruit the help of a neighbor, who just so happens to be the secret slasher.

346. Create a scenario in which a bitter ex-cop dons tactical gear and then begins to mimic the work of an urban slasher. They do this because they are convinced that if they "stop" these murders, they will be welcomed back to the force with open arms. However, this will have consequences the ex-cop never saw coming.

347. Instead of a headless horseman, a modern rider uses night vision goggles beneath a hood. He gallops along country roads, slicing at unsuspecting drivers with a cavalry saber. In the morning, deep hoofprints lead to battered car doors and the echo of galloping hooves, far too real to be folklore.

348. Write an unusual scenario in which your character helps an urban legend slasher. How did this happen? What does the "help" consist of? Further, what happens to your character when the slasher no longer needs their assistance?

349. A group of teens dare each other to sleep overnight in a cemetery, convinced that a slasher roams amongst the graves at night. After a few weeks, the teens get bored when nothing happens. That is because the slasher has moved on—to the attic of their high school.

350. Your character wakes up in a cold, dark room to the sound of beeping. Still groggy, it takes your character some time to realize they are in a medical facility. Their back hurts just below their ribcage, and your character lets out a low groan. Little do they know, they are down one kidney and are being kept alive for a group of slashers that need a few other organs.

351. "Aren't you glad you didn't turn on the light?" Your character is startled by the message, written in blood, and soon they find their roommate's cold body. It is clear this is the work of an urban legend, but unfortunately, nobody believes your character's claim.

352. Deeply inspired by the Candyman legend, your character has decided that they will be the next slasher. Of course, this is not going to be without severe consequences. Craft a story that deals with this urban legend slasher's infamy and their eventual downfall, leading to a life behind bars.

353. Choose a cultural urban legend not yet featured in this book and create your own slasher twist on it. Be sure to include a character that also has no respect for local customs.

354. Your character stops to grab breakfast before driving another 95 miles before stopping to get gas. This will be a long road trip, but your character is determined to make it to their grandparents' house before nightfall. After another 145 miles, they pull over for lunch at a remote diner. Your character is utterly oblivious to the stranger who has been crouched in the backseat the entire time.

355. Turn the "Babysitter" urban legend on its head. A babysitter receives several ominous phone calls repeating, "Have you checked the children?" This urban legend usually ends with a call to the police and their response that the call is coming from inside the house. This time, suppose that instead of the police being called, the stalker calls back and, in a horrified voice, screams, "Oh my God! What have you done to the children?" The babysitter smiles evilly.

356. Jeff the Killer exemplifies how urban legends evolve to fit the current generation. Originating on message boards and then social media, *Jeff* has finally died out and is regulated to deep dive videos. Suppose a series of online posts resurface and those who read these posts late at night receive a handwritten note that only reads," Go to Sleep."

357. Your criminologist character is studying serial killers inspired by local urban legends. Choose a legend from your hometown and weave it into the story, using this myth to craft both the criminologist and the serial killer character.

Holiday Hellscapes

While most holidays certainly include good cheer and fellowship, they also create an increase in stress and, for some, homicidal tendencies. The following writing prompts exist at the corner of joy and terror, amplifying every scream and lining seasonal backdrops with blood.

358. Surrounding the town hall, underneath a bright night sky, glittering confetti flies through the streets along with a mass of people. New Year revelers are counting down with rosy-cheeked excitement. A masked figure is also watching the clock and intends to use the booming fireworks to mask a killing spree.

359. "What's your New Year's Resolution?" Your character receives this strange note on their door and immediately throws it in the trash, assuming it's some kind of advertisement. It isn't. Your character has been selected for a slasher whose resolution is to beat the previous year's body count.

360. Imagine a scenario that takes place during Chinese New Year. Amid the swirl of lion dances and fireworks, a cloaked figure slips crimson envelopes into the pockets of unsuspecting attendees. Usually, these envelopes symbolize good luck and prosperity, but letters from this stranger only symbolize bad luck and death.

361. Rose petals litter the walkways across the campus. What should be a time of love and romance is about to turn sinister. On a nearby rooftop lurks someone in a Cupid mask. Armed with a bow and arrow, this slasher targets couples they deem unworthy of love. What qualifications do they go by?

362. Write a story that involves horror but a touch of romance. Your character's love was murdered on Valentine's Day, and now, a year later, your character is hunting the slasher – who is now hunting their next victim.

363. As couples waltz under chandeliers at a sweetheart's masquerade, a hidden hand locks the doors, trapping attendees inside. Shortly after, a masked dancer slips between couples, bearing a sharpened rose stem with which they intend to paint the ballroom floor with blood.

364. Colorful beads and loud throngs of people flood the streets of New Orleans as Mardi Gras mania gets underway. Someone wears a carnival mask somewhere in the crowd, but unlike other slashers, this person is looking for someone specific. Who are they looking for, and what do they intend to do once they find them?

365. Mardi Gras did not originate in New Orleans but in Mobile, Alabama. A disgruntled resident is tired of people wrongfully attributing the birthplace of this famous holiday to the wrong city. As a result, this hunter abducts people from The Big Easy and takes them to Mobile. For what evil purpose? That's up to you to decide!

366. Holi is known as the Hindu festival of colors. It marks the beginning of spring, good harvests, and, ironically, the triumph of good over evil. The slasher in this scenario celebrates through only one color — bloodred.

367. Your slasher character is frustrated about their chosen holiday - St. Patrick's Day. They have been doling out their own form of punishment for years, but it has become too easy. With green beer flowing, the pub crawlers practically run into the slasher's knife. Why has this slasher chosen this holiday in the first place? Further, what happens after the slasher becomes disenfranchised by the ease with which they can kill?

368. Known as The Good Luck Killer, a slasher allows potential victims to decide their fate each St. Patrick's Day. Some roll dice, some try to pick a four-leaf clover, and so on. What game of chance does your character play, and what will fate decide?

369. Write a scenario in which pranks turn lethal on April Fools' Day. These characters don't necessarily start as slashers, but when these pranks continue to escalate, their evil sides finally bubble to the surface.

370. "All Fools Must Die," the masked killer cries as they raise a knife over your character's head. "Wait...wait," your character shouts, "I'm no fool...and I can prove it!" How do they go about proving it?

371. Children dash across lawns, cracking colorful eggs that reveal small, bloodstained notes inside. Where do these cryptic clues lead, and who is behind them?

372. Write a horror comedy in which the Easter Bunny takes revenge after their basket of eggs is smashed by unruly children at a gathering in the park. You can decide if this Easter Bunny is a disgruntled employee in a costume or if it is the literal holiday rabbit.

373. Imagine a scenario in which your character goes on an Easter Egg hunt that leads them further and further away from their family and friends. Each egg is filled with money, and the denominations get bigger and bigger until your character finds the last egg deep in the forest. That's when a person wearing a rabbit mask appears, carrying a loaded shotgun.

374. Everyone gathers in the park to celebrate yet another Earth Day. Attendees are joyous, as plenty of vegan dishes are being served and free saplings are given to take home. But laughter turns into screams when several polluters are strung up in the trees by vines that serve as makeshift nooses. Who is responsible for this?

375. "What I require is blood and roots." A masked slasher roams Arbor Day, looking for a new victim who will serve a sinister purpose—from their body, new trees will grow.

376. Write a scenario that involves a mother-in-law from hell. This should be a story that escalates - for example, at dinner, she stabs the steak just a little too hard, and then later, your character is given a "gift" that looks suspiciously like a human heart. Will your character survive the night?

377. A charming Mother's Day brunch is shattered by an axe-wielding parent. What is the reason behind this slasher crashing the event? Are they a former parent who no longer has a child? Is this a custody battle? Just what is going on?

378. It's prom night, and attendees begin to cough and hack before falling

over dead. It seems someone has poisoned the punch bowl. Who is it that has committed this dastardly deed, and why?

379. A killer has been targeting the senior class, and your character suspects they might be next. It's up to them to find the killer's identity before no one graduates this year.

380. Your character passes their yearbook around for their classmates to sign before the end of the year, but they do not look at who signed what until they get home. When they arrive and skim the pages, they see an odd name—a student who died their freshman year. Is this a sign of a ghostly encounter, or is a slasher toying with them?

381. Against the sea of outdoor grills and "Kiss the Chef" aprons, a slasher slinks around the Father's Day block party. They plan to wait until night when they can get revenge on the father who failed them and anyone who might stand in the way.

382. Write a sinister horror story in which a serial killer poses as an unassuming dad each Father's Day, targeting those who do not have a father figure in their life. Your character is one such person who has just been abducted, but this slasher has pegged them all wrong. Your character did have a father – a survivalist who taught them all the skills they would need to escape this nightmare.

383. Your character is set to attend a summer solstice celebration. They have never met many of the attendees, and the person who invited them is a little cagey about what to expect. When your character arrives, they find a big pig being roasted on the spit, only it isn't a pig.

384. Write a story in which a slasher is the inadvertent hero. During a Fourth of July celebration, this slasher plans to kill a few partygoers while the thunderous explosions ring out. Before they do that, they see a "true patriot" targeting people who they deem "Unamerican." This slasher finds their first victim and is praised for their heroism for taking this person down.

385. Your character and their family are invited to a barbeque by a distant cousin for a Fourth of July cookout. When they arrive, your character is surprised to see the fire going but no meat on the grill. That's because your character and their family are supposed to be the main course.

386. Your character wakes up and finds that they are strapped to a bunch of cylinder objects that smell faintly like sulfur. When the music begins to play, and the ceiling parts to reveal the night sky, your character realizes with horror that they are strapped to several large fireworks. Who is responsible for this soon-to-be gruesome display?

387. Imagine a horror story in which a disgruntled employee returns to the office on Labor Day to take revenge on a narcissistic, awful former boss. However, the boss is expecting this former employee and has set the entire office building up to be filled with one booby trap after another.

388. Families gather at the beach for one last taste of summer on Labor Day. When they try to make their way back home, they find that the town bridge, the only road back, has been destroyed by a bomb. It seems a secret killer has trapped them and intends to pick them off one by one.

389. Your character cowers in an alleyway, their white pants stained from blood and sweat. "No white after Labor Day," a cruel voice whispers before the chainsaw can be heard again.

390. It's time for students and teachers to return to school, but this year's orientation has a horrifying twist. The principal has gone rogue and has set traps throughout the entire school. Now, students and teachers must work together to survive this deadly game of cat and mouse.

391. When clocks spring forward—or fall back—a paranoid slasher believes society is stealing their life's

hours. Marking each victim in sync with the clock shift, the killer scrawls "Time's Up" near the bodies as the hour hand jumps.

392. A slasher has been using the time change to increase their kill count, primarily targeting victims in the darkened morning or early evening hour. Your character is the only one aware of this pattern and has decided to take it upon themselves to catch the killer. Little do they know, they are the next target.

393. Envision a scenario in which Columbus Day, now known as Indigenous People's Day, is marked by a serial killer who picks people off one by one. Why? For still celebrating the holiday's former intention.

394. A suburban street bustles with costumed kids. They're invited into one neighbor's darkened home for a "special scare." In the morning, the children have gone missing, and all that is left are bloody candy buckets, each representing an echo of "trick or treat" that have gone silent.

395. A slasher has a rather unusual but still horrifying way to kill their victims. Every Halloween, they leave a package with a note that reads "trick" on the doorstep of their chosen victim. Inside is a caged rabid bat. It might take a while for the disease to set in, but when it does, it is the slasher who gets the "treat."

396. Create a horror narrative where your character is trapped inside a haunted house on Halloween. They know that there is a real-life slasher amongst the skeletons, zombies, and other Halloween jump scares. What your character doesn't know is that there isn't just one.

397. A truth-or-dare game on Halloween goes horribly wrong when the dares keep escalating, and the truth reveals deeply disturbing secrets.

398. Your character and friends attend a Halloween murder mystery party for someone they have not seen in years. The initial body, set to start the mystery, seems a little too realistic. Then, the first attendee dies. The guests were brought because of what they had done for the host all those years ago.

399. November 1st through November 2nd marks Dia de Los Muertos, a Latin American holiday that honors deceased loved ones. Among colorful altars and sugar skulls, a silent figure in skeletal face paint hunts celebrating families. Why does this slasher go after these specific people?

400. Each *Día de Los Muertos*, your character kneels against their *offrenda*, lighting candles and placing down items each person might have liked in life – certain snacks, a can of their favorite drink, cigarettes, etc. No portrait is in sight and instead the withered faces of each of their past victims line each row.

401. During the day, a small town celebrates a harvest festival where families delight in pie-eating contests and hayrides. Everyone quickly retreats to their homes at night, hurriedly locking the doors. Those who do not make it back will be hunted by a slasher known as The Scarecrow King, who kills amongst the cornfields.

402. Your character and their fellow guests are enjoying a delicious Thanksgiving meal, unaware the host has sinister plans for attendees. The turkey isn't the only thing that will get carved tonight.

403. Aside from eating turkey, Thanksgiving dinner is usually a time for sharing gratitude – and airing grievances. Someone clears their throat and stares right at your character. "I know about your little secret. It's time everyone knows, too." Your character is a slasher responsible for the recently reported murders. How do they respond to this comment?

404. The host clears their throat. "Today, I just want to say I'm thankful for each of you." The guests, who are all bound and gagged, begin to cry.

405. It's Black Friday, and a group of shoppers have already formed a line outside the megastore at dawn. Once they are allowed to enter, they find the exits are all locked. Over the loudspeaker, a voice says, "We're happy to announce we have replaced our normal Doorbuster Deals with... Headbuster Deals." Employees emerge from the backroom and march towards the aisles, each wielding a baseball bat.

406. Cyber Monday is traditionally held after Black Friday when shoppers get access to online deals. One special online coupon has a computer virus attached for anyone who unwittingly interacts with it. Now, the slasher not only knows the locations of potential victims, but they can also access their computers and any smart device.

407. Write a Hanukkah horror story in which a body turns up each night of the week. From somewhere, deep in the seedy underbelly of the city, a slasher lights a menorah afterward, knowing what they have done. The real question is, why has this slasher chosen this holiday in particular?

408. All through the house, not a single creature is stirring except for - a slasher. This killer creeps around victims' homes, drinking milk and eating cookies left for Santa. Thus far, no one has been murdered, but that is because the slasher is waiting. What - or who - are they waiting for?

409. A family sits in the living room, happily unwrapping Christmas presents. It is tradition for them to dig into the stockings afterward. When they do, your character will get a horrifying present - a photo of someone they killed and buried. Which family member has discovered your character's dark secret?

410. Write a Christmas horror story inspired by a century-old tradition - ghost stories. Your story should include a ghost story, whether it involves an actual ghost, or this is a story within a story, and a slasher who will stop at nothing to get what they want.

411. Strangers glance at the person wearing a Santa mask with some caution. Christmas is over, and this person continues saying they are Kris-Kringle. That's because this slasher believes that Santa gets to pass judgment all year, and those found guilty must pay the ultimate price - certain death.

412. For this story, research the traditions and celebrations behind Kwanza. Then, write a horror story in which, each night, the next victim's house is marked with symbolic candles. The cause of this selection? Cultural betrayal.

413. It's Boxing Day, and your character has several wrapped parcels ready to go to some of the less fortunate people in town. Little do they know, one of these "less fortunate" is a wealthy individual disguising themselves to make it easier to prey on people for this special day.

414. For some, certain events that occur each year can be considered a holiday. For example, Ren-fair goers cheer knights and jesters each year while eating a bounty of good food and enjoying other Medieval entertainment. Your self-described "Dark Prince" character is amongst the crowd, using their costume as a cover to lure their next victim.

415. An annual farmer's market is filled with fresh produce and florists who want to display their year's work. Create a rivalry between two slashers, a gardener who releases tiny venomous insects in their crops and a florist whose roses have thorns dipped in poison. Who will win this strange battle?

416. For many, cruise season is a holiday all on its own. Especially when new themes are announced. Your character is a slasher who also gets excited about this annual tradition. Armed with their trusty harpoon and binoculars, they set up on the dock and take aim.

417. Throughout the year, there are several animal adoption events, from those centered on special holidays to more general themes that simply wish to clear out shelters. Among the attendees is a zealot slasher who believes humans are the real monsters and wants to save animals from those they deem unworthy.

418. One of the most significant nonholiday traditions is the many sporting events that take place each year—from wrestling tournaments to football games. Choose a sport you are familiar with and create a slasher who has become the coach of a famous sports team, ensuring that they can pick off players they hate individually.

419. Once a year, the school gym transforms into a stage for the annual talent show. Many budding artists are eager to show off their unique skills, but among them is one unhinged performer who shouldn't even be there. Humiliated in the past, this person returns with a new act - one that will silence any critic that dares to boo.

420. Balloons and confetti set the stage for a surprise birthday party. Everyone is crouched behind furniture in the semi-darkness, wearing smiles and stifling giggles. That is until the laughter turns to blood-curdling screams. The guest of honor has arrived, and unaware that anyone is in their home, they also are dragging the body of their most recent victim.

421. A sweet 16 turns sour when the lights flicker, and the DJ stops spinning tracks. A masked figure emerges from the giant gift box, complete with pink and purple bows, turning the dreamy night into a sinister and deadly performance.

422. A *Quinceañera* is a Hispanic tradition that celebrates a girl's 15th birthday. There is often a religious ceremony and individual traditions (like gifting a last doll), followed by a large celebration. Another tradition is added at this celebration – the girl will kill her rival in cold blood.

423. For this horror story, create two characters that are a couple and choose what anniversary they are celebrating. No matter if it's their first year, golden, or somewhere in between. Now craft a scenario in which a past lover returns and is finally ready to enact a vow made long ago, aided by a sharpened blade.

424. Create a scenario in which a character is retiring after 50 years of working at the same company. Instead of the pension they believe they are getting, complete with a going away party, they only find a bag of candy and a note that asks them to turn in all their keys and equipment by the end of the day. Now, your character will throw their own retirement party, and the bosses they invite will not be going home after.

425. Each year, relatives gather at the old homestead for photos, potluck dishes, and forced smiles for the annual family reunion. One black sheep cousin has arrived with a cryptic scrapbook detailing family secrets. They also carry something else—a knife sharpened by decades of resentment.

426. Choose a holiday, event, or celebration not covered in this prompt book. Once you find your find selection, include a story with the following: someone obsessed with a specific date, a conflict involving

three people, and a slasher who cannot be stopped.

427. Write a horror story that spans an entire year. A self-declared holiday hater turns slasher targets every holiday that comes along. By the middle of the year, this slasher has already killed several people, and by the end of it, the tables will be turned on them. But how?

Survivors & Sequels

The final confrontation might end in triumph for those left, but that does not mean the nightmares stop. Far from it, oftentimes, the killer's demise only creates an unshakeable sense of dread and the fear that true evil will never be contained. These prompts show that survival becomes a lifelong battle when one tries to overcome the worst humanity has to offer.

428. Your character is a therapist who specializes in serial killer survivors who now have PTSD. Your character is good at what they do, but they have started making a name for themselves. As a result, they get on the radar of a few killers

who will stop at nothing to seek information on those who got away.

429. "Every nightmare ends – until it doesn't," a friend tells your character, who was hailed a hero when they ended a killer's reign. Now, fresh murders echo the same pattern, and it seems like the nightmare has indeed come back.

430. In horror films, the final girl is a trope referring to the last survivor, usually a female who confronts the killer. Create a horror story that uses the final girl trope but creates a twist. For instance, the final girl is the killer, or it is revealed that the killer is related to her.

431. Years after escaping a slaughter, a medical intern is now a pathologist working in a morgue. A body comes in that looks exactly like their former tormentor. Panicking, they go home, take a breather, and return the next day to work on the body, which is now gone. Instead, a message is scrawled on the slab: "You're next, Doctor."

432. Decades after their ordeal, survivors stand together to watch the house where they were tortured and chained be torn down by the city. Everyone cheers and celebrates except for one person. The evil fiend, never caught, stands in the back, watching their home be destroyed.

433. Write a scenario in which a survivor dedicates their life to tracking down other killers. Eventually, they become just like the killers they catch. How does this escalate throughout the story?

434. Years after the original rampage, a string of new murders erupts in the same small town. Police suspect a copycat until the battered survivor recognizes the killer's voice behind the mask. It seems the killer has not only returned but is eager to get revenge.

435. Confined to a secure psychiatric hospital, an infamous serial killer no longer speaks and just stares at the wall in their room. That is, until the killer is about to die, and when they do, they confess a dark secret, one that involves the last victim and the actual person behind all the murders.

436. Imagine a scenario in which your survivor character comes home to find a package has been delivered to their doorstep. This large gift contains a tarnished machete with a note that reads, "For the next time."

437. Plagued by survivor's guilt, one victim attends group therapy only to meet someone who seems to know a little too much about the killings' intimate details. As the sessions continue, your character becomes painfully aware that this person is more than an empathetic listener, but they might be part of the original slaughter.

438. Your character has noticed a strange pattern in a ring of reported murders. It looks like what your character escaped from years ago. What your character doesn't realize is that the killer, right before they died, unleashed a legion of copycats.

439. "You've come back to the crime scene," a voice sneers from the darkness. "A place that you knew was my domain." Your character is scared, but they have come for a specific purpose – to kill this monster once and for all.

440. As part of the recovery process, the final survivor begins vlogging about their trauma. Cryptic comments start to hint at unknown aspects of the murder, underlining that one of the lurkers might have been there that night. The real question is – are they the killer or a secret witness?

441. Determined to conquer their fears, the last witness to a killer's rampage embarks on a hike through the same woods. Halfway along the trail, they find fresh carvings in the trees—signs that someone is hunting them again.

442. "Return to Blood Lake if you want to know why it happened." Your characters' hands shake while they read the anonymous letter left in their mailbox. Does your character decide to go? Furthermore, who sent the letter?

443. Write a scenario in which a cult uses black magic to resurrect a savage slasher who once terrorized an entire town. The cult believes they can use the slasher for their own gain, but this plan soon backfires.

444. Your character has practically lived in their panic room after being abducted by a killer that resulted in a nationwide manhunt. Your character starts to feel safer years after the incident and begins to return to normal life. That is, until five years later, when the surveillance feed shows a familiar face prowling around the yard.

445. "What made you think it was just one killer?" Your character gulps at the detective who has just spoken. This is the first time they hear such a question; now, they rack their brain for an answer. It should have been obvious, but it wasn't. It seems there are more killers out there.

446. Your character has outsmarted the masked killer, and now they are trying to lead a normal life. This is going to be rather tricky because every relationship always ends the same – with their romantic interest dying in an accident. As it turns out, the killer has returned and targets those closest to your character.

447. Decades after a double homicide, a witness tries to renovate the family home where the killing took place. It was always understood that the murderer was caught, convicted, and placed in prison. The story changes, though, when polaroids are found in hidden compartments, which suggests that there was not only a third murder but the killer isn't who they thought it was.

448. Your survivor character receives a notice that they have named in a stranger's will. Unaware of any inheritance, your character arrives at the probate office, where they learn they have inherited a large estate. Of course, this is all a ruse for the killer, who has set a series of traps in the mansion for the one who got away.

449. Your character has finally started walking the neighborhood again after they were brutally attacked on the street just a few blocks from where they live. En route to their home, they spot a missing poster with a photograph that looks unnervingly like the person who attacked them. Has the killer gone missing, or is your character now being stalked and taunted?

450. After a string of horrific slayings, an imprisoned killer is interviewed by police with the hope that it will help them crack the case. As a result, the cops are murdered, and the slasher escapes, now looking for the key witness that put them away in the first place.

451. Write a scenario in which the killer is actually angry at the mercy the victim has shown. For months after the incident, the victim receives the same sinister phone voicemail, "You let me live, and now you must die."

452. The killer is dead. Now, your character wants nothing more than to put that horrible ordeal behind them. Then your character catches a news story about a missing-person report; some elements are eerily similar to the original slasher's MO. Is this a copycat, or is the killer still alive?

453. Your character escaped a run-in with a slasher but still carries scars and insomnia. Each night, they see a familiar form in their dreams, always coming closer and closer. When they wake, the injuries that cover their skin suggest the nightmares might be a little too real.

454. For several months, your character has had strange nightmares about the person who almost killed them, now buried in the local cemetery. They just cannot shake the feeling that something is wrong. Despite others calling them crazy, your character finally goes to the graveyard and starts digging. The coffin is empty.

455. After a harrowing car chase that ended in a crash and the killer's fiery death, the lone survivor can't drive this route without reliving the night. Tonight seems to be different, and they have a strange sense of calm while they take the path, unaware that the reanimated killer is now in the backseat.

456. The rural site of a legendary bloodbath is resurrected as a new "rejuvenation" retreat. One terrified survivor sounds the alarm on how disrespectful this is, but no one listens. On opening day, ominous footprints appear around the luxury cabins, mirroring the killer's old routine.

457. Your character has been invited to give a survivor talk to a group of criminology students at a university. While your character speaks about surviving the blade of a serial killer's knife, they suddenly see that very killer in the back row, watching intently.

458. The survivor of a summer camp massacre sits in the attic, going through old photos of friends who died long ago. Then they find a picture of a friend who moved several states away and changed their name after the incident.

Attached is a handwritten note in blood that reads, "Looks like I forgot one." Your character must find this person before the killer goes after them both.

459. Craft a horror narrative in which a Hollywood director adapts a survivor's story into a film. The survivor is invited to sit with the director and crew during an open casting call. Towards the end, someone resembling the killer steps in front of the camera. When the survivor looks closer, they realize this is indeed the person who tormented them long ago.

460. Suppose that two survivors from two separate mass murders connect online. They form a deep bond over their shared trauma, perhaps even a romantic one. Before long, both receive a letter stating, "If you unite, so do we."

461. Your character is now in the witness protection program and has finally adjusted to their new life. Before long, however, someone begins leaving ominous messages that hint that the dreaded slasher is back.

But that seems impossible. After all, your character is the one who killed them in the first place.

462. Write a story in which your character has completely capitalized off the mass murder they survived. They have gotten movie deals, book deals, and multiple speaking engagements. In reality, your character wasn't even close to the slaying, and now they are in danger of being found out when the slasher returns.

463. Create a rather disturbing narrative in which a victim's child was taken and never seen again. Now, the slasher has not only returned to seek vengeance on the person that got away but also has additional help, the survivor's own child turned against them.

464. A slasher has escaped from prison and decides to lay low – sort of. They begin recruiting copycats who will wear similar wardrobes and masks, each promising to follow the MO strictly, or else they will share the same fate as the killer hopes the survivors will.

465. A burned high school is all that is left from a tragic accident where several people have died. Decades later, the building is finally torn down, but it reveals bodies that were dead long before the flames lit. It seems a killer was overlooked, and now that they might be found out, they rise again.

466. Tormented by ongoing PTSD, a survivor begins to see the dead murderer's reflection in every mirror rather than their own face. Is this an example of the killer returning from beyond the grave, or of a slow descent into madness from extreme trauma?

467. While on a podcast, the lead investor who closed a serial killer case years ago breaks down specific facts and an insider look into the criminal mind. As the broadcast goes viral, something the detective says piques the interest of one of the original survivors, who is now convinced that the person charged and tried is innocent and it is the detective who is the real killer.

468. Imagine a scenario in which a cruise liner was the site of a horrific murder of over 200 people. The killer was finally apprehended and tossed overboard, assumed dead. A few of the survivors are invited back to the grand reopening, and on the first night, they all complain about the same thing – they can sense the killer's presence in every dark corner of the ship.

469. "Do you still forgive me?" The killer sneers. Your character, once left for dead by the same murderer, has completely changed their life around after the horrible ordeal. In fact, they have gone on what they call a forgiveness tour, giving lectures about the power of letting go and moving on. "Do you still forgive me?" The killer repeats. How does your character respond?

470. A group of murder survivors band together to hunt down the killer when the police force drags their feet on the case. What they learn is that someone in that same force has been helping the killer the whole time. Are these survivors successful in bringing both to justice?

471. Craft a scenario where two survivors meet over coffee, convinced that their crime scenes look too similar to not be brought on by the same killer. This kickstarts their exploration of a dark, underground crime ring where murder is livestreamed.

472. A social shelter welcomes survivors of violent crimes, hoping to give them a fresh start. But when personal items vanish, and a telltale symbol is scrawled on walls, it's clear that one "survivor" is actually there to finish what they started.

473. When a joke shop begins selling masks bearing the killer's likeness, your survivor character has had enough. They have already dealt with movies, books written from an outside perspective, and even T-shirts with the killer's face on them. What does your character do to combat the issue?

474. Your survivor character holds the hand of the killer they once escaped from long ago, who is now on their deathbed. With the last bit of energy, the killer leans forward and whispers a cryptic message before dying. What did this killer say, and more importantly, how did your character come to care for them when they could barely escape from them a few decades earlier?

475. Create a horror narrative in which a slasher has hired an apprentice to take revenge on survivors while they serve their time. You can take this story from the perspective of the survivor, apprentice, or killer who only gets periodic updates.

476. Your character has begun living off the grid deep in the forest out of fear. After a decade, they become entirely accustomed to the lifestyle. Then, they find strange footsteps around their encampment and dark messages carved into trees. The killer has found them again, but your character is ready this time.

477. From the perspective of the survivor, dive into a criminal trial of a mass murderer, which your character survived. Primarily focus on the fear of giving their witness testimony and the potential for the killer to take revenge during or after the trial is over.

478. Your survivor character sharpens blades, fills explosives, and fills gas in their getaway car. The killer, responsible for the murder of their entire family, has been sent to a psychiatric hospital that is known for its resort-like nature. Your character plans to ensure the killer gets the justice they deserve, no matter what consequences may come.

479. Your character finally finds some sense of solace when the murderer is locked away, but then they happen to run into the killer's new pen pal. Without letting this person know who they are, your character manages to get information about an upcoming escape and, perhaps more horrifying, revenge plans against your character.

480. A local church organizes a candlelit vigil for those killed in a small-town massacre. A single survivor joins in on the hymn, uncomfortable with the attention but thankful for the community. As they sing, they recognize something off about the priest – a small scar on the bottom of their chin, which is suspiciously like that of the killer they escaped from.

481. After surviving a slasher's attack, a theatre troupe comprised of survivors performs a drama based on the ordeal, hoping that it offers catharsis. Right after the opening night performance, when the lead actor is supposed to take their bow, they go missing. Instead, someone writes *Encore* in blood in the dressing room mirror backstage.

482. A visually impaired survivor, made that way by the killer, still carries memories of the contorted faces screaming in terror. Now, it seems someone has begun leaving notes in braille at their door, detailing aspects of the murder no one else would know. It looks like the killer is still taunting this survivor, but this time, the survivor refuses to be a victim.

483. Your character buys a box of miscellaneous computer equipment at an old garage sale. Amongst the collection is a flash drive. When your character plugs it in, they find a video diary detailing a murderer's thoughts on each victim. Your character recognizes the case because it was in the news. Based on these tapes, your character also realizes that the person charged with the crimes is innocent.

484. Suppose a last survivor has been haunted by phantom phone calls, weird text messages, and even targeted emails – all marked by the name of the killer. Is this an example of the survivor's own continued psychosis from their trauma, or is it a result of a returned killer?

485. Your character and a group of friends decide to summon the spirit of a slasher by performing a ritual over their unmarked grave. Nobody in this group expects it to work, but it does. Perhaps a little too well. The slasher has been restored to flesh and is now looking for their first victims, who are right in front of them.

486. Quite disturbingly, it is not uncommon for slashers to garner admirers while in prison. This can be romantic advances, business proposals, and everything in between. Suppose a slasher uses one of these admirers simply to harass previous victims, and as a result, this adoring character will have to face dire consequences for deciding to dance with the devil.

487. Your character is a prison guard who notices the dead body in the cell, alerts supervisors, and then transports the corpse to the morgue. That's when the killer attacks. It is up to your character to fight the slasher off, or they will be responsible for this monster escaping and targeting their previous victims.

488. While most of these prompts deal with the killer going after their direct victim, slashers can also live on in other ways. Craft a scenario in which a slasher had a child before they were killed, and now that same person, now-adult, is going after who is responsible for the killer's death – your character.

489. "Say you remember me, and I'll let you go," The slasher taunts your character. Yes, your character has had a run-in with this killer before, but because of trauma and amnesia, they don't remember it. How can your character get out of this scary situation?

490. Your character combs through the newspaper in what should otherwise be a dull morning. Suddenly, they see their name underneath the headline, "Massacre Killer Returns After Twenty Years." With shaking hands, your character gulps, unaware that the killer is somewhere in the house.

491. Imagine a scenario where your sibling character is the sole survivor, leaving behind their twin. Decades later, your character notices that every mirror seems to have a lingering glance, and every window's reflection has too intense a glare. It's almost as if the twin has returned, seeking vengeance for the sibling who left them behind.

492. Your character is a sheriff who found the bodies, hunted the killer, and reassured the town that the nightmare was over. But was it truly over? Investigating another similar case, your character begins to doubt whether they got the right person.

493. The blood is all your character can remember from that night at the party. Waking up without a memory of anything else, they're met with fascination from some but terror and unease from others. Trying to piece together what happened, many are hesitant to talk openly about that fateful night – until the killer returns.

494. "I saw them die. I know I did." Ten years after a mall massacre that horrified the nation, your character, an accomplice, gets off on account of an error, releasing them from their life sentence. However, once out, they come face to face with someone who should be long gone.

495. Having survived an almost-murder in the woods, your character vows to stick close to the trail. White knuckling their mace spray, a scream rips through the forest. Now, your character is stuck at a crossroads. Should they risk their second chance at life or help ensure another gets theirs?

496. Your character is turning the town's worst tragedy, an accidental fire that destroyed numerous homes and lives, into a movie. But as production begins, the sound stage is set ablaze. The actor's houses and apartments are in ashes, and costumes and scripts are burned in a pile. Was it as accidental as they all thought, or is it someone wanting the notoriety for themselves?

497. *A brother?* Your character would remember having a brother, wouldn't they? Knowing nothing else after the brutal murder of their parents, your character is constantly sent family photos showing someone who clearly has familial ties. Your character assumes it is Photoshop, but it isn't. They do indeed have a brother, and this person may have been responsible for deaths years ago. That begs the question – what do they want with your character now?

498. A survivor writes a best-selling memoir about escaping a serial killer. However, after a grueling book signing and hours of meeting and greeting numerous fans, your character finally notices that someone has placed a weathered and beaten copy of the book on the table. Baring scribbled notes in the margins and a note that reads, "it's not over."

499. Getting out alive was only the beginning of survival for your character. Craft a story about their return to normalcy, from the physical and psychological therapy they must endure to what happens when the killer inevitably returns.

500. Your character smiles and leans back in their chair, proud at having finished their book. A work that will hopefully help other slasher victims who have gone through what your character has gone through. Suddenly, there is a crash, and a dark figure crawls through the window.

COMING SOON

500 Horror Writing Prompts: Circus

ABOUT THE AUTHOR

Hailing from Houston, Texas, Christina Escamilla is a genre author who focuses on short horror fiction that blends the dreadful with the introspective. While her work can sometimes be considered macabre, it is still a lens that she uses to explore the human condition.

Beyond her fiction, Christina enjoys crafting writing guides and prompt books to help the next generation of writers. When she isn't writing, you can find her hiking wayward paths, exploring oddity shops, or haunting a coffee shop.

Learn more at stinaesc.com

www.ingramcontent.com/pod-product-compliance
Ingram Content Group UK Ltd.
Pitfield, Milton Keynes, MK11 3LW, UK
UKHW041322270425
5650UKWH00031B/323